ADVANCE COMMENTS

"David is a superb naturalist, an uninhibited storyteller and vivid word painter of landscapes, wildlife and people whose fun memoir will leave you learning and laughing."

— Lyn Hancock, well-known author of many popular books, including *Looking for the Wild*, *Tabasco the Saucy Raccoon* and *There's a Seal in My Sleeping Bag*

"A rip-snorting tale for those who prefer the extraordinary over the mundane. David Stirling's lively account of a two-year-long motorcycle odyssey among the wonders of Australia and New Zealand is sure to quicken the blood and impel you to pursue your own dreams."

— Alan MacLeod, birder-naturalist and sometime wayfarer among the wonders *Down Under*

"An insightful and interesting read about travel and nature in the lands Down Under *post World War II."*

— Bill Merilees, naturalist, writer and tour leader

OTHER WRITING
BY DAVID STIRLING

David Stirling has written many scientific and popular notes and articles for various publications including *The Canadian Field Naturalist*, *The Murrelet*, *The Victoria Naturalist* and *Stitches*. He has co-authored *A Naturalist's Guide to the Victoria Region* with Jim Weston, *Birds of British Columbia* with David Hancock, *Pacific Wilderness* with David and Lyn Hancock, and *Where to Find Birds in Canada* with Jim Woodford.

BIRDS, BEASTS
AND A BIKE
UNDER THE SOUTHERN CROSS

DAVID STIRLING

Agio
PUBLISHING HOUSE

ACKNOWLEDGEMENTS

My thanks to Barbara Begg and Alan MacLeod
for drawing my attention to my bad spelling after
reading the first draft of this manuscript. More
thanks to Alan for scanning pictures, drawings and
documents. Thanks to Ursula Vaira of Leaf Press
for a professional editing.

PUBLISHING HOUSE

151 Howe Street, Victoria BC Canada V8V 4K5

For information and bulk orders, please contact
info@agiopublishing.com *or go to*
www.agiopublishing.com

Contact the author at dstirling@shaw.ca

ISBN   978-1-897435-19-9 (trade paperback)
        987-1-897435-20-5 (electronic edition)

10 9 8 7 6 5 4 3 2 1 a

Printed on acid-free paper made without fibre from
endangered old-growth forests.

This book is dedicated to Ruth who shared these adventures.

Ninety Mile Beach, New Zealand, 1956.

The first draft of *Birds, Beasts and a Bike* was typed by Ruth
in 1960 from the copious notes I made along the way.
Nothing has been changed, except for a few bits
that here and there refer to the present.

"...If you haven't got to travel, you might as well stay at home...
I mean the inner necessity, which drives a person to travel though it
may be against his more facile inclinations, against discretion, against
the will of others: to travel when he can't afford it, when he is not fit
for it, when it means sacrifice and insecurity... This is the kind of
travel I have in mind, the kind of travel that is done when one can't
afford to travel at all, when one is taking the risk of being stranded
somewhere... It may be the traveller's intention to return
when some of his curiosity has been satisfied, when his urge
to see other countries and people have been appeased."

—Rupert Croft Cook, *Seeing the World*
courtesy of William Hodges & Co. Ltd.

"The world is a book and those who do not travel read only a page."

—Saint Augustine

TABLE OF CONTENTS

BIRDS, BEASTS AND A BIKE

PROLOGUE

The *Ghan* has arrived in Darwin, the realization of a dream first envisaged in 1859. One of the longest rail lines in the world, stretching from Adelaide on the Southern Ocean, nearly 3,000 kilometres to the tropical shores of the Timor Sea at Darwin on Australia's northern tip, is now a reality. No wonder all the dignitaries were present, and in true Aussie style a group of men and women were flashing their breasts (women only) and mooning the 1.5-kilometre-long iron monster. Cheeky smiles all round. I wish I had been there – to see the train arrive.

Way back in 1958, I rode the *Ghan* from the terminus in Alice Springs to Port Augusta, Adelaide's sea port. The information about the tracks being extended north from Alice to Darwin was exciting to me, as I am a bit of a train buff. *Ghan* is an Aussie shortening of *Afghan*

Aussies moon historic arrival of new train

The Daily Telegraph

From the
TIMES COLONIST
Wednesday February 4 2004

SYDNEY, Australia — The first passenger train to cross Australia from south to north arrived in Darwin on Tuesday to be welcomed by women flashing their breasts and men baring their backsides in a mass "moon."

It was not the reception expected by the dozens of dignitaries, including a former prime minister, Gough Whitlam, who had travelled for 47 hours aboard the 1½-kilometre-long train from Adelaide.

"There were about 60 of them all lined up," said a photographer, Clive Hyde. "That's the Outback for you — you're pretty much free to do what you want. The girls were flashing their boobs left, right and centre. The coppers asked the men not to flash their dangly bits," Hyde said. "I just hope it didn't put the dignitaries off their food."

Police asked the group to keep away from a gathering of local families who were also awaiting the arrival of the "Ghan," named after the Afghan camel handlers who helped explore central Australia in the 19th century.

Traversing nearly 3,000 kilometres of desert, scrub and sand dunes, the Ghan is the longest north-south railway in the world, the realization of a dream first envisaged in 1859. Until now it had extended only as far as Alice Springs, half-way across the continent.

The first passenger train to travel the length of Australia's newly completed south-north railroad is greeted Tuesday by thousands of cheering people in the northern port of Darwin.
Mike Corder /Associated Press

referring to the Afghan drivers who steered long camel trains though the desert back in the gold rush days.

Seeing this recent newspaper clipping set me to remembering the two years of travel adventures that Ruth and I experienced under the Southern Cross in the 1950s. Soon I was tidying up my notes and pictures to create this book. I hope you enjoy it.

❀

Our trip began in western Canada in the mid-1950s, back in those pre-historic days before television, political correctness, metric, computers, bank cards and cell phones; even before crash helmets, gay marriages and plastic shopping bags. Half a century? With all the technological and social changes of the past fifty years, it seems more like a full century. We – my wife Ruth and I – chose to leave the daily round of toil and the accumulation of worldly items (not that we had any at that time) for the open road and adventure. A pilgrimage to see some of the world's natural wonders, from pointy mountains and stormy skies to leafy trees and feathery birds! We would travel around the world beginning with an extended stay in New Zealand and Australia. Not many birders were tramping the earth in those days for the pure enjoyment of avian delights. It was well before mass tourist air travel and before the world's highways and byways were macadamized and clogged with unwashed bodies toting backpacks, and globetrotters backed up by TV camera crews.

The decision was not easily made. Canadians had been through the Pioneer Years, the Great Depression and a long war known as WW II. Now the economy was good; social services were arriving from Ottawa. It was the best time since Confederation to dig in, consolidate, hunker down and get a house with all *mod. cons.* Television, not yet available, was on the eastern horizon. Friends and relatives were negatively unanimous: "Settle down; get a government job before the next depression begins. They [the omnipotent *THEY*] are giving returned service men job preference." I was a *returned man* with five years overseas service.

"Go for a job now," our kin advised. "Sit on your arse for thirty years and then go on a pension." Good advice. Perhaps down the road in a few years? For us, adventure beckoned although we didn't have a pot to pee in or a window to throw it out of. How would we afford it?

I learned to ride and enjoy the motorcycle experience in England during WW II. The British-made Norton [*Snortin' Norton*] was the Canadian Army's choice. Often a lethal one too. An often repeated rumour was that Hitler said, "The best way to deal with the Canadians is issue every soldier a Norton and they will all commit suicide." I am sure Hitler never said anything resembling that. He probably wasn't too concerned with Norton bikes or even the Canadian Army at that time, but it illustrates how important we considered ourselves.

For me, a bike seemed to be the ideal vehicle: in touch with nature, unlimited vision, the elements in your face and you could haul ass far over the horizon on a gallon of gas.

My birdwatching began one bitter winter's day back on the homestead at the edge of the boreal forest north of the town of Athabasca, Alberta. I was twelve. Peering through a clear hole in a ice-caked windowpane (space made by concentrated hot breath and finger nails in order to see out; like an Arctic seal's breathing hole), I watched a party of fluffed up Black-capped Chickadees trying to find dormant insects in the shaggy bark of nearby fence posts. I was concerned. My father suggested I place some rolled oats – staple food for both man and beast – on the nearest post. The chickadees were grateful. Later, I established a feeding station in the scant shelter of the winter-nude aspens behind the house. Rolled oats, wheat and meat scraps brought in Grey Jays, Blue Jays and Magpies. I scattered weed seeds and wheat on the hard snow on my daily tour to the chicken house and barn for hungry groups of tiny redpolls and scintillating flocks of Snow Buntings. Spring brought a confusing array of sparrows and warblers. The blue sky was streaked with V's of fast-flying garrulous geese and gliding trumpeting Sandhill Cranes. Silent, mostly solitary, Golden Eagles and Rough-legged Hawks were heading north to the Yukon. I was hooked. I was now a birdwatcher.

Many years later I became a *birder*, leading nature tours worldwide, seeking birds on the high seas and enjoying great spectacles such as the fall migration of storks and eagles crossing the Bosporus in Turkey, the Saskatchewan sky sparkling horizon-to-horizon with Snow Geese, and the 5,000,000 individual birds of the *River of Raptors* over Cardel, Mexico.

Meeting the Ghan again in 2003
for the Indian Pacific journey from Perth to Adelaide.

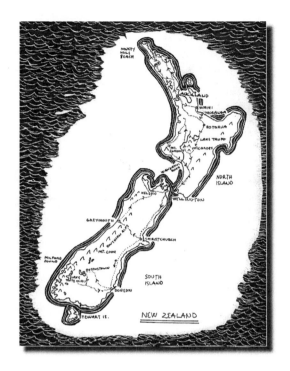

1

PRUNING TREES WITH MR. TAPTOES

We are on the road again, this time south of the Equator. The roar from our 350 cc Ariel motorcycle, overloaded with the necessities for a projected long camping journey that would take us from Ninety Mile Beach in the north to Milford Sound in the south, is destroying the tranquillity of the New Zealand morning. At last we are off on our great adventure.

The previous year, Ruth and I rode two BSA bikes from Athabasca, Alberta, over the freshly constructed Hart Highway, linking British Columbia's Peace River Triangle with civilization down south, to

Abbotsford in the Fraser Valley. The *improved roads* were gravel, tire-deep on the Hart; dust and small stones for miles. The choking dust was almost solid when churned into horizontal tornadoes by passing cars and big rigs.

Arriving in British Columbia's Okanagan country, we stopped to acquire some much-needed cash by picking fruit. Here we met Dennis Dann, an adventurous Londoner, on a BSA Bantam and in the same impecunious state as we were. The three of us settled into a rustic shack and tied into the Macintosh apple harvest in order to build up our monetary reserves. It was a fine outdoor life, climbing about like bears in those big old trees, with ever-changing views of blue mountains and green valleys. We lived high on inexpensive fruit and vegetables and paid no rent. It was a carefree summer even though our only water was running cold from an outside tap and the sanitary facility was an antique bum-full outhouse.

On the Sabbath, we explored, by bike, the old logging trails, the Kettle Valley and Washington State. The ferocious Kettle Valley road was all gravel – mostly boulder-size stuff. Once we had to spend a night in an abandoned shed, with a family of friendly pack rats using our sleeping bags for their rest stops.

Our *Down Under* travels began in April when we left Canada. The fifteen-day voyage across the Pacific, on the old *Orion* from San Francisco, was restful and pleasant, but the skies were grey and wet in Auckland, for it was winter in the Antipodes. We planned to stay, travel and enjoy nature for perhaps two years in New Zealand and Australia before returning home. When our money ran out we would take whatever employment was available. With these objectives in mind we would purchased a motorcycle and camping gear in Auckland.

Since it was winter we decided to work in Auckland until spring. Employment was easy to get in those days. Ruth settled into the office routine in the country's largest department store; I went to work

BOY IT'S WET OUTSIDE!

BELOW: Cargo workers "in the dry" watch seamen and shipping company men handle baggage in the rain. ABOVE: Passengers waiting for the rest of their baggage to turn up.

From the
AUCKLAND STAR, NZ
Monday May 14 1956

pruning trees for Auckland's parks. Unlike employment, accommodation was rare and expensive. After several unproductive days of walking the streets, we found one large room in a rambling frame house within speaking distance of Mt. Eden Gaol. On Saturday afternoons we were entertained by the soccer game commentary on the prison's loudspeaker while inhaling the scent of mash and hops from two great breweries dominating the skyline.

The winter was wet and colder than we had expected. The little two-by-four fireplace was not able to heat our large room even with the unlimited supply of free wood that was one of my perks from tree pruning. In the evenings, Ruth, working the knitting needles, produced two fine sweaters which helped us make it through the chilly months.

The park's tree and clean-up gang was a pretty congenial lot. Pruning street trees meant climbing about in the street trees like Orangutangs, one hand for hanging on, the other for hacking off unwanted branches with a hook-billed, razor-sharp slicer. When we weren't pruning, we planted trees and shrubs in city parks and boulevards. Another job was cutting up and removing the big trees that came to an inglorious end in savage winter storms. Good open-air exercise. Work attitude was rather casual. Only *smoke-o*, the morning and afternoon tea and smoke breaks, was sacred.

One morning a new employee joined our group. As he was the youngest of the gang, only a teen, he was referred to as *the boy* or *our boy*. He was a keen worker but a champion risk taker. Once, taking a swipe at an unwanted hunk of vegetation while perched high in a crack willow (an English import) there was sharp report. The willow branch had not only cracked, as it was supposed to do, it had broken clean off leaving our man sprawled among stronger wood ten feet closer to the ground with his nose sniffing a thick power cable.

Then there was an official occasion at a city park. We had a load of trees and shrubs to be planted after the speeches, and the ceremonial trees were duly earthed. Just beyond the dignitaries our boy was noticed selling plants to the spectators, at cut-rate prices, from the tail-gate of the truck. Fortunately for the ceremony, the misappropriation of city vegetation was stopped before the truck was totally defoliated. Our boy's excuse: There were far more shrubs than needed and he was going to donate the money to the smoke-o fund. A self-motivated business man and a philanthropist. A born winner. He would, to quote the old cliché *go places.*

The boy had a habit of falling dead asleep at smoke-o, so dead that it was necessary to give him a stiff elbow or a sharp boot in order to bring him back to reality. At that time we didn't know he had a B&E business on the side. Finally, one morning, the boy failed to show up for work. Next day there was a news item in the local paper: Mr. *Taptoes arrested.* Two teens returning home late from an evening school class put on a rock music (just invented) disc on the record player. Soon they heard a loud tapping noise. It was coming from under the bed. A discreet peek revealed a prone man, asleep but keeping time to the music with his number-twelve boot. The teens phoned the police, kept the music blasting, and our boy, Mr. Taptoes, was off to the slammer. On the pruning gang, work and smoke-o went on at the usual pace.

The Maori name for New Zealand is *Ao-tea-roa,* land of the long white cloud. During the winter of 1956 an endless procession of these long white clouds, moved over Auckland, borne on the west wind blowing over the Earth-encircling southern ocean. Over the Waitakeries, a range of hills west of the city, their bottoms dropped out, soaking us. The approaching roar of raindrops on the city's acres of tin roofs drowned out the traffic noises. In the intervals between showers there was brilliant sunshine and often a crisp rainbow in the south at noon. We seldom had one of those grey, drizzly days that are a common feature of winter in coastal cities of the Northern Hemisphere.

The continuous washing of the atmosphere and the high convection produced a clear sharp sky that was ideal for star-gazing. In August, Mars made its closest approach to the Earth in seventeen years. At the end of the month another unusual event occurred. In the morning the planet Venus was plainly visible after sunrise. This would not occur again until the year 2140 AD. By keeping a close watch on this planet I was able to see it with the naked eye throughout the day from sun-up until late afternoon. As might be expected, radio stations received numerous calls from people reporting flying saucers. One caller, perhaps a tea-cup-and-saucer researcher, said he hoped the sceptics were finally convinced: non-believers need only to look up and see a real one.

On our voyage steaming southward from California, we had watched the Southern Cross rise higher while Polaris dropped lower in the north. Near the Tropic of Capricorn, the Big Dipper, that constellation so familiar to northerners, dropped below the Earth's bulge. As I watched the sky at the bottom of the Earth I found the constellations of the Zodiac looking entirely different. How strange was the shape of Orion from this angle; the Hunter was hanging head down in the north. I was looking up at the moon's pock-marked South Pole. The southern Milky Way was a sky-dominating delight with its nebulae, Coal Sacks and Magellanic Clouds.

Living and working in Auckland got us dovetailed into a new way of life. We lurked among the books in the public library, met a random sample of *Kiwis* and joined in the meetings and nature rambles of the Forest and Bird Society. Sorting out the birds was easy but we got hopelessly bogged down in the vegetation. We visited parks and the magnificent museum in the Domain where we were fascinated by a reconstruction of the Moa, the world's tallest bird. We went on a charter fishing outing in Hauraki Gulf and hiked up Rangitoto, that recently extinct cinder pile in Waitemata Harbour.

In August we bought a second-hand 350 cc Ariel bike for sixty-nine pounds, a good chunk of our money in those days, and sallied forth on some major exploratory trips. We visited Bethels Beach and Muriwai Beach where the long swells of the Tasman Sea break over black volcanic sands. We explored the mud flats of the Manukau where thousands of shorebirds – godwits, stilts and Wrybills – spend the winter. The godwits arrive in thousands from Siberia; the stilts and Wrybills are natives. We found the mud flats flanking Auckland's motorway to be a fine place for a quick binocular scan for cormorants, black and pied, Australian Gannets, White-fronted and Caspian Terns, White-headed Stilts and White-faced Herons. Out on the harbour: Giant Petrels as big as Albatross beckoned.

The Waitakeries was the place to make the acquaintance of the North Island's semi-tropical vegetation. We found fine examples of Kauri, Rimu, Manuka and Puriri. Down near the beach we saw extensive groves of Pohutukawa that thrive best in the salt-laden air. Magnificent tree ferns, some up to thirty feet in height, filled damp gullies.

A lazy Sunday afternoon often found us on one of those bubble-like cinder cones which are a feature of Auckland's landscape. Now grass covered, they supported flocks of *woollies*, New Zealand's favourite animal.

It was October and spring in the south. The days were warmer but it still rained. The English Oaks in the Domain were bursting into pastel green in contrast to the dark olive green of the native vegetation. The dawn chorus of introduced birds – Song thrush, Dunnock, Blackbird, Green Finch and Chaffinch – rivalled that of spring in England.

Our preparations for our Grand Trek intensified. We gathered our gear for a self-sufficient motor-cycle trip that would last several months and take us from Ninety Mile Beach on North Island to Milford Sound in the far south. We piled up a change of clothing, toilet articles, notebooks, flashlight, groundsheet, two sets of knife, fork and spoons, mugs, plates, two nesting billy cans with lids, frying pan, tire repair kit, hunting knife, whetstone, collapsible canvas bucket, water bottle, sewing kit, plastic bags, fishing tackle, sleeping bags and sheets, some light rope, first aid kit, machete, maps and identification books – birds, plants, southern night sky, geology – the *Rubaiyat* of Omar Khayyam, binoculars, cameras, extra film, exposure meter, telephoto lens and a magnifying glass. We stuffed the tool box with extra nuts and bolts, spare clutch cable, a spare spark plug and some necessary tools.

The only field guides available at that time were pretty inadequate and bird-finding information, bursting the shelves now, was unheard of in those days. It was ninety-nine percent *do it yourself*. We had to make do with some pretty rudimentary stuff, which meant we had to observe more closely and work harder to put the proper names to birds and plants. Ruth would carry a shoulder bag for our lunch grub – the *tucker bag*. All this plus two persons was a rather overloaded 350 cc rig. It was OK on the scarce bitumen but treacherous on backcountry gravel and dirt. But, with the personal guidance of Saint Christopher and very careful riding, we would log seven thousand miles in New Zealand, and later ten thousand miles in Australia without serious trouble.

We are ready for a weekend shake-down trip to Port Waikato, fifty miles out of Auckland. The bike was unwieldy at first but when out of the city and puttering along in the sunshine beside the willow-choked banks of the Waikato we had balance and steering under control.

We rode over grassy limestone hills stiff with sheep and cows. Charred stumps, the decaying remains of giant trees, and patches of tree ferns and manuka in the gullies were reminders of the forest that was. A glade of tree ferns hiding the entrance to a large cave beckoned us to pitch our tent and *brew up*. Ominous storm clouds and a freshening north wind brought early darkness. There was time for a short visit to the cave.

With flashlight in hand we walked in on the greasy floor beside a little stream. Our light flickered and failed leaving us in the darkness of the pit. The blackness and silence was total. But there were tiny pinpoints of light above, all around and even beneath our feet. Glow-worms. In this silent, dark world it seems that we were viewing the constellations of the heavens from a point in space where the stars were visible from above, around and even below, for pools of water on the floor reflected the stars on the roof. We stood enchanted in this fairyland not daring to speak for fear that the stars would disappear. Later we found that glow worms are not easily frightened but this was our first encounter with the luminous denizens of caves and grottoes.

Glow-worms, *Arachnocampa luminosa*, are the larvae of a two-winged insect similar to the crane fly. These larvae can be found in caves and shady, damp banks usually over pools of water. The steady light they emit from the rear end attracts gnats on which the worm feeds. The gnats are caught on gummed threads that the glow-worm has draped around itself. When the lunch is secured the glow-worm slowly sucks up the thread with the attached meat.

Next day we explored using a light rigged up on the motorcycle battery. It is a young cave as caves go and, although wet and dripping, only baby stalactites and stalagmites have formed. About a kilometre underground, we came to several branch tunnels and cave-ins where candle smudges on the walls marked the past presence of other spelunkers. Time to back out.

2

BELLY UP IN THE KAURI TREES

Near Ruakaka we pitched our tent on a grassy bank overlooking the finest white sand beach we had ever seen. After an overnight drizzle, the next day dawned clear and warm. There were a few puffy clouds in the clear blue sky and little waves from the South Pacific tinkling on the shore. What a day for leisure and absorbing a few rays. While enjoying the perfect weather we got an overdose of sun. My nose looked like the Pope's nose on a well-done Christmas turkey. A week later we could have passed for a pair of eucalyptus trees – our skin peeled off like strips of bark. While getting burnt we watched birds. Godwits and knots were arriving from their breeding grounds in northern Asia, some with injuries sustained on their long journey south. Both South Island

Pied and Variable Oystercatchers were common and we noticed that the two species did not associate with each other. Australian Gannets and Great Cormorants fished just a few yards off the beach. I thought some plunge-diving gannets must have struck bottom but I didn't notice any with corkscrew necks.

We moved on to Whangarei where a reporter from the local newspaper, the *Advocate*, found us, then to the Bay of Islands, famous for big game fishing. We stopped to taste the famous grapefruit from Kerikeri's citrus groves then on to Doubtless Sound and Ninety Mile Beach where the pounding surf sounds like a thousand-gun artillery barrage. Later, we rode through the Mangamuka Gorge to Opononi where just a year before our visit, Opo, the friendly dolphin, played in the shallows with bathers. Press and radio made her a celebrity. Her fame spread until one day she returned no more. Later she was found dead, wedged between some rocks. The theory: she was killed accidentally by fishermen who use the surefire gelignite fishing method.

In the Waipoua Forest we stood in awe under giant kauri trees. The kauri belongs to an ancient plant family, *Agathis*, which predates the northern hemisphere's pines and firs by God knows how long. Close relatives range around outpost lands of the southern hemisphere. The kauri is the undisputed queen of southern hemisphere trees as these vital statistics of one of the last remaining demonstrates: diameter – seventeen feet; age – 1,200 years; log content – 214,000 board feet. The taperless trunk rises limbless for a hundred feet. There are tales of a kauri that measured thirty-one feet in diameter. The largest authenticated tree measures twenty-two feet in diameter; truly the kauri is the arborescent matriarch of the Antipodes.

The New Zealand forests are completely different from those of the northern hemisphere. Viewed from above, the scene is a rolling mass of spreading crowns; humps rather than spikes. The kauri, in particular, sends up a massive trunk before the huge limbs fan out like mighty umbrellas. Its smooth, grey trunk looks like a granite column.

It rained again. The road was heavy gravel, almost cobblestones, and

A Kiwi.

each stone had a skin of slime. We slithered broadside on the slippery surface and capsized, becoming a jumbled pile of canvas bags and a bike wheels up with us on the bottom. Momentum and grease kept us moving until we came to a sudden stop, ass over teakettle, in a water-filled ditch. The slippery slope that caused the accident most likely saved us from serious injury, as there was no resistance to our unorthodox, upside-down progress. We escaped with only minor bruises and a bad shake-up. Our rig sustained a bent footrest and a flattened exhaust pipe.

The shelter and fireplace in Trounson Park was a godsend that evening. What joy it was to sit by a blazing fire and choke down mugs of scalding tea while the heat penetrated our wet clothes and aching joints. Later, while Ruth tended the fire, I walked out in the sylvan wonderland under the massive boles of kauri and into an open glade where the setting sun illuminated a mosaic pattern on the topmost branches; below all was in darkness. A Tui tinkling unseen in the treetops only added to the silence. Here was the primeval forest, a relic of the past. I wandered the forest glades until stars twinkled through holes in the forest roof. My reverie was terminated by a weird, shrill "kee-wee," then an answering "kee-wee" from close by and yet another. I was in the middle of a Kiwi concert. I imagined a family of quaint creatures with hairy feathers and long beaks probing the humus for earth worms and other succulent morsels in the dark world under the great trees. A description of the Kiwi is hardly necessary as it is widely known as a symbol of New Zealand and a brand of shoe polish. A rude person described the Kiwi as a long-beaked, flat-assed duck. The Kiwi is still moderately common in parts of New Zealand, but being nocturnal it is rarely seen. The only one we saw was a captive in the Auckland zoo.

Now the night shift came on duty. I heard the harsh rasping of a weta, a mega-cricket. Then a pair of Morepork owls began a duet. Few birds are as aptly named as the Morepork. From dusk to sun-up and from forest to suburban garden, this medium-sized owl emphatically calls for "more pork." The *Ruru*, as the Maoris call it, has likely increased since the coming of European settlement as new prey species such as mice, rats, sparrows and starlings are numerous.

Groping my way out of the forest, I missed the track. I stumbled over roots and got tangled up in ferns and vines. I blundered around in the undergrowth and squelched in the mud. My sense of direction, usually good, had failed me. I was cold, bruised and confused. I was almost resigned to thrashing about all night. At last I found a track and by starlight I set off hoping that this was the right direction. By sheer outhouse luck it was the path back to the fire. Home sweet home. Ruth had the billy on and we had another bout of hot tea.

3

ORAKEI KORAKO

We met Hank and Jop, their three kids and big dog Caesar at Wai-hi Beach. Hank and Jop had a unique but smelly occupation. As the town had no sewers or septic tanks, someone with a strong back and a weak nose had to collect and empty the night jugs. Since most of the town's citizens had turned up their noses, Hank and Jop got the job only after driving a hard bargain with the city fathers. Every evening, properly dressed in rubber suits, they mount the tank wagon to pick up and empty brimming buckets at a shilling a pail. They were looking forward with keen anticipation to the coming holiday season when the resort's population would increase ten-fold. To quote Hank, "There's gold in them buckets." The job was the right one, for Hank, a keen surfer, had the day free to loaf on the beach and respond to "Surf's up." Jop, of course, had the kids and tending the house.

Riding down to Rotorua we nearly ended our journey before it had really begun. On a straight but narrow road a beat-up car approached on the wrong side (NZ's right side). I hoped the driver would realize his and our plight and move to the left. I moved over onto the edge and slowed down but the other guy kept his course. Jaisus! He was out to get us! I was only inches from a deep water-filled ditch, when the car shot past. A wide-eyed chuckling maniac at the wheel poked his head out and shouted "Chicken!" I shouted an appropriate oath and contemplated changing my underwear.

The vast thermal regions of New Zealand are world famous. Perhaps the greatest concentration of boiling mud, blowholes, hot springs and sulphur pits in the world is found around Rotorua and Taupo. Whakare-warewa (usually condensed to *Whaka*), a tourist destination near the town of Rotorua is the site of a traditional Maori village. There are other less-commercialized, and for us more-interesting, thermal places. Each site has its own special characteristics. Wiatapu, on the Taupo highway, is famous for its sulphur pits, champagne pools and paint pots. Wairakei is the site of a major geothermal project.

We planned to explore Orakci Korako where there was no commer-cial development and no signs to warn visitors from disappearing into sulphur pools or getting fried on natural barbecues. With us were Peter and Margaret, a Canadian couple also touring by motorcycle, and Bill. Bill was a bit strange: a neurotic character, but a cheerful, inoffensive neurotic. We would not have met Bill if it hadn't been for a series of gusty winds and rain squalls that drove us into the kitchen shelter of the tourist camp. Bill, like us, under cover keeping dry, soon became an unshakable companion. This was his first holiday alone. It appeared that he had been under the absolute control of a domineering partner for the past twenty years or more. Now unleashed, he was *out for adventure,* preferably of the amorous kind. He had optimistically brought an extra camp cot and a bottle of special wine in case he got lucky.

Bill had a thing about frequent costume changes: from a greyish T-shirt and shorts to a colourful shirt and shorts, and back again, especially if he had an audience. Between garb changes he paraded in his underwear.

Bill insisted we should leave our bikes at the camp and go to Orakei Korako in his car. It was a nice gesture but we were stupid to accept. We were barely on the road when we realized that we had made a mistake. In New Zealand it is customary to drive on the left. Bill preferred the right especially when negotiating blind corners which made up the whole road. If that wasn't enough, he had the disconcerting habit of making eye contact with the back seat passengers while keeping up a steady yakking. Bill's yakking consisted of a long history of his accidents. He had done it all, from driving over an embankment to ramming a parked car while operating a vehicle without brakes and lights. Of course it was the fault of the other guy, the weather or even wrongly-placed traffic lights. Bill eventually got the idea that we were not happy with his driving, only after we mildly announced our concern with several outbursts such as, "Watch the road!" We had to be firm but we didn't want to hurt his feelings.

After Bill succumbed to our advice, we were able to enjoy the scenery, which consisted of a wide belt of pumice-desert country sprouting coarse tussock grass, and manuka or tea trees now in a delightful mist of white blossoms. On a pumice knoll a small band of brumbies – feral horses – watched us. (Perhaps they weren't truly wild, but it made us happy to think they were.)

Arriving at our goal, we found that we had to cross the swift Waikato River on an old-style ferry that was propelled by the current. The ferryman, an amiable chap, wanted to go to town. It was Saturday, his afternoon in town, and he had a lifetime of boiling mud and stinking sulphur behind him. "You chaps can handle the ferry. Anyway there won't be anyone else out here today," he said.

N.Z. MOTOR CYCLIST 1/-

JANUARY, 1957

★

Edited by . . . .
AUDREY HENDERSON,
23 Merritt Street,
Whakatane.

I have recently had the pleasure of meeting four of the best ambassadors Canada could possibly have in New Zealand. Ruth and David Stirling and Margaret and Peter Davel arrived here last May and after working in Auckland for the winter set out last November to tour our country as part of their proposed world tour. Wherever they go I am sure they can't fail to leave behind them a feeling of happy friendship.

Whilst they were in the Rotorua district I had the pleasure of meeting Ruth and Margaret a number of times and we had some very interesting chats together. Although they both come from Victoria, B.C., Canada, the girls did not meet until they had almost reached New Zealand on the Orion.

Purchasing two machines after riding two-up and carry particu- their arrival here both couples are larly bulky loads. The Stirlings

Ruth and David Stirling all ready for an early start.
N.Z. MOTOR CYCLIST

16

ride an Ariel and the Davels an A.J.S.

Their plans really appeal to me in that the two parties are making no attempt to travel together continuously. This saves any possible clashing of plans and they can keep in touch with each other and meet in some of the principal centres.

It was in this way I was fortunate enough to meet both couples at the same time. They both set up camp at the Rainbow Springs Motor Camp, Rotorua, each party having its own pup tent, sleeping bags and cooking utensils.

Touring is nothing new to Ruth and David who have already ridden many thousands of miles in Canada on two Bantams. Until her marriage some five years ago Ruth had done no riding and rather startled her parents and friends when she and David began their wanderings. She says that motor cycles are used almost entirely for sport in Canada and U.S.A. and are not seen on the roads to the extent they are here. English machines are particularly popular there. About a year's planning went into this present tour and an approximate route was worked out prior to arriving here, although it was not possible to settle any details as maps and general information about N.Z. were difficult to obtain. Apart from motor cycling Ruth's interests include bird-watching; photography; knitting and horse riding. She is certainly finding plenty of scope for the photography during this tour and already she and David have a comprehensive range of colour slides which they hope to show publically upon their eventual return to Canada.

Margaret and Peter Davel were planning to visit Peter's home in South Africa when they decided to see as much as possible of the world on their way. Going by New Zealand's position on the map and the scant information they could obtain they felt that the climate should be ideally suited to motor cycling and the country would be interesting to visit. So far it has

19th JANUARY, 1957.

been much cooler than they had anticipated but nevertheless they are pleased they decided to make the visit.

Prior to this tour Peter had done quite a deal of riding, principally on a Triumph Twin, but it is Margaret's first taste of the sport and she is thoroughly enjoying it. Like Ruth she finds the trip offers plenty of scope for her interest in photography.

Since their arrival both parties have ridden up north as far as Kaitaia and are now heading towards the south. Margaret and Peter riding down the east coast and Ruth and David down the centre of the island. They expect to meet again in Wellington.

All four are high in their praise of our N.Z. sign posting. They find it clear and easy to follow.

Riding on the left instead of the right-hand side of the road did not take long to become accustomed to but they do find it difficult to get used to looking right instead of left when out walking and stepping off the footpath to cross the road.

Margaret Davel beside a well-laden mount.

17

After giving Peter and me a few basic instructions on ferry handling, he waved goodbye and shouted, "Take your time and enjoy."

Across the river we found a thermal wonderland. Mud pools ranging in colour from dirty black to pure silica white bubbled and plopped like cauldrons of stiff porridge. The white stuff was talc smooth; the dirty stuff was coarse and unpleasant. In some mud pots a stiffer mixture produced miniature volcanoes that gurgled and sent up plumes of steam. Basins of water, some ice-cold, some boiling-hot, covered much of the ground. Yellow was the dominant colour, but some pools were deep blue, some vivid green and others even bright red. Waterfalls turned to stone were silica terraces; their overall whiteness streaked with the yellow of sulphur, red of iron oxide and the green of algae that thrives in hot water. Underfoot was a thin skin of white silica with vents spewing steam and hot water. I wondered how thick this shell was. It was scary. Were we being stupid wandering over the roof of Hell? But it was so fascinating. Bill, who was usually only an elbow away, had disappeared. Had he broken through the crust? Perhaps he was already shaking hands with the Devil.

We entered Aladdin's cave, a tremendous vault lined with rock of fantastic colours. Below, a tepid pool produced a faint sulphurous mist. Standing beside the pool, whose far shore was invisible in the gloom beneath a million tons of rock, we looked back toward the entrance. The mouth of the great cavern was garnished by the fronds of tree ferns against a background of azure sky. Here the Earth in all her omnipotence and serenity would humble the most arrogant human.

We were silent, each with his or her own thoughts. Our reverie was shattered by a wild yell and a strange echoing splash, "Come on in, the water's great!" Bill had fallen in and was flinging his soaked clothes in the direction of the shore. Perhaps he was down to his underwear again, or perhaps beyond that. He was still with us. It was time to leave.

The Rotorua-Taupo scene was reminiscent of North America for here were forests of pines utterly different from the native New Zealand vegetation. The pumice plains and volcanic hills were disguised by vast

Watch your step!

coniferous plantations, chiefly Monterey Pines, usually referred to as *radiata* the specific name from the Latin, *Pinus radiata*. These plantations, perhaps the biggest in the world, were the mainstay of a thriving wood industry. Lake Taupo with an area of two hundred and forty square miles is the largest lake in the country. The lake's blue, translucent waters rival those of the Mediterranean. From its north end the Waikato River begins its winding journey to the southern ocean.

We spent several shivering nights in the rain on Taupo's shores, compensated somewhat by the musical croaking of the introduced Australian frogs and the *booming* of the Australian Bittern, a natural concert from the neighbouring reed beds.

What drew visitors from all over New Zealand to Lake Taupo? It was not the booming of the bittern, the blue waters or the landscape of pines. It was the fabulous trout fishing. Trout, like many other species brought here by man, had found this new habitat to be much better than their original home. In the absence of natural predators they grew faster, fatter and more abundant than they had in their native land. One of our fondest recollections of Taupo – next to, of course, frog music, booming bitterns and natural hot baths – was trout fishing. Excellent eating too.

Riding up from Tauranga through pleasant farming country, we reached the summit of the Kaimais. Before us lay a grand sight: a hundred miles away the symmetrical, active cone of Ngnauruhoe and the snow-covered, massive truncated Ruapehu filled the entire southern horizon. But it was only a glimpse for within minutes the scene was shut down by a curtain of mist and cloud. Perhaps a quick view is more indelible.

We approached the great mountains over the *desert* road. The desert is a plateau of ash and pumice deposited over the ages by numerous volcanic eruptions of both lesser and greater magnitude. The road was straight and much favoured by *speed artists;* the vegetation was tussock grass and tea-tree shrubs. Narrow belts of southern beech forests outline the tracks of winding mountain streams.

We entered Tongariro National Park via the back door, and continued past the chateau to a clearing in the beech forest where we bivouacked for the night. And what a night. Above us loomed the snowy pile of Ruapehu, around us the deathly-silent beech forest, over the entire world the magnificent southern stars. Next morning while huddling over a smoky fire we prayed for a sunny day after an absolutely bone-cracking cold night. We must have done the proper rites for the sun rose clear and warm. With the sun came the cheery tinkling of foraging Bellbirds. We were now able to appreciate our awesome surroundings.

Looking north we saw a plume of smoke rising from the crater of Ngnauruhoe, its snowy flanks dirty with new ash. Beyond Ngnauruhoe was flat-topped Tongariro which gave its name to the national park. Westward, across sixty miles of rolling pastoral country, a line of flat-topped cauliflower cumulus marked the shores of the Tasman Sea. Eighty miles away in the southwest, a perfect white volcanic cone rode high in the heavens, seemingly floating above the earth. This was Mt. Egmont, an 8,260-foot extinct volcano, second only to Mt. Fujiyama in symmetry and beauty. It is not connected to any main mountain range. Here was

On the slopes of Mt. Egmont.

the best view of Egmont. Seen from the south it has a secondary cone, Fantham's Peak, which spoils its symmetry. Approaching New Plymouth from the north we saw Egmont again floating in the sky, but because of the configuration of the land, Egmont was now floating over the blue Tasman Sea.

We decided to have a day on the slopes of Mt. Egmont. The sky was clear and sunny. We hiked through the glorious native bush on the lower slopes where we saw lumps of volcanic material stuck in the crotches of ancient trees. Perhaps extinct is the wrong term to describe Egmont. We reached the scoria slopes at higher altitude and after a restful appreciation of the scenic menu we noticed clouds rapidly congealing about us. It was time to back-track to a lower elevation. Beauty and isolation give Egmont an aura of benignity that has contributed to the death of several climbers. Like most mountains it is a weather maker, and its scoria slopes are dangerously unstable.

New Zealand is a land of volcanoes. White Island, rising from deep water twenty-seven miles off shore in the Bay of Plenty, is noteworthy. Only four miles in circumference, White Island is the scene of spectacular thermal phenomena. The sulphur deposits were worked for a while until 1914 when an eruption blew the whole establishment including the staff of eleven men to oblivion. Since then no attempt has been made to start a new sulphur operation. A good view of the smoking heap can be obtained from Parry's Lookout at the summit of Mt. Ngongotaha near Rotorua.

In June, 1886, Mt. Tawarewa blew, burying the village of Wairewa under twelve feet of mud and ash. One hundred and fifty-three people were killed; ash covered over five thousand square miles. The partly-excavated village has become a tourist attraction. A remarkable feature is the row of large poplars that have sprung up from the village fence posts.

Peter and Margaret had just pitched their tent when we arrived in the cow paddock near the Waitomo Caves. It had been a broiling day riding through the King Country and although my nose was as red as a gobbler turkey's neck, it was great to enjoy the sun after the numbing cold and rain of the previous week. At the caves, the major tourist attraction, there was only a hotel for the moneyed visitor and a shabby kitchen-washroom for the impecunious travellers like us.

Visiting the Waitomo Caves did not give us that sense of adventure we felt when exploring the dark limestone vaults at Port Waikato. Here, electric lights were installed at the entrance and a guide was required. Nevertheless, it was exciting experience. Huge wetas lurked in dark grottoes. Not the sort of thing you want down your neck. These insects, up to fourteen inches long, are mostly spiky legs and antennae, adaptations for life in total darkness. They are nocturnal vegetarians venturing outside at night and retreating to the cave's shelter for the day. Beyond the guardian wetas we were in a remarkable wonderland of stalactites and stalagmites. You can remember what goes up and which goes down by: "the mites go up the tites come down." Variety, colour and formation defy description and yet there is more around the corner – the glow-worm grotto. In the guts of the earth we boated slowly along an underground river where a million tiny lights shine all around. In the silent darkness, glow-worms were everywhere.

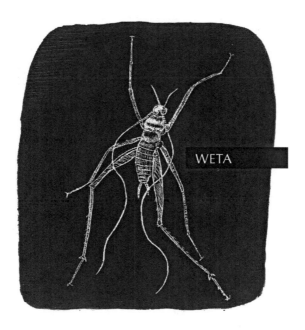

WETA

4

UP THE CREEK ON THE WANGANUI RIVER

We floated down the Wanganui, a 150-mile-long river, that begins in the mid-island's volcanic plateau and finishes in South Taranaki Bight, at the city of Wanganui. Downriver from Taumarunui, where we embarked with a flotilla from the Auckland canoe club, there are ninety rapids. Sheer rock walls with dripping ferns and moss rose up on either side of the canyon's rim. An exciting roar from hidden cascades reverberated from dark, vegetation-choked clefts where water has worn cuts back from the main river. Along a narrow ribbon of sky, eight hundred feet overhead, grey and fractured clouds rested on the matted treetops. From this nimbus, thousands of feet thick, torrential rain poured down on us soaked and shivering individuals who had chosen

Merry Christmas, 1956.

to run this river of rapids, snags, overfalls and record high water in the worst kind of weather in a tiny rubber dinghy. The canoe club members would float swiftly in kayaks and a canoe. Peter, Margaret, Ruth and I, tagalong adventurers, were given this floatation device: a small inflatable rubber raft and four paddles. We got the idea we had been invited along to transport the bulk of the expedition's supplies. The dinghy was bottom heavy with cardboard boxes of Creamota breakfast cereal, cans of herring and a gigantic wheel of cheese. Perched on the dinghy's edge, water lapping against our bottoms, feet up on the cheese, we contemplated our folly. We were intruders in a world of overpowering vegetation and suffocating water.

In preparation for the river run, we had arrived in Taumarunui, the pushing-off place, on December 24. In a quiet cow pasture on the outskirts of town we prepared to spend Christmas Day lazing in the sun. Tomorrow, the river. In keeping with the season we had decorated our tent with fern fronds and bought the best lamb chops for a big fry-up. But we had not reckoned on Maori hospitality. On Christmas morning while strolling in the suburbs we came upon a group of Maoris preparing a *hangi*, a native-style feast, where the food, an unfortunate pig with the trimmings, is covered with green leaves and cooked underground on hot coals. The original pressure cooker. We were invited to dinner, a mid-day feast. We couldn't refuse. The lamb chops would have to wait, perhaps; without refrigeration, they were already *off*. What a feast! Roast pork, a plethora of fruit and vegetables, Dominion lager, wine and champagne. Several families were present. A steady stream of relatives and visitors moved in and out. This was only the beginning, we were told. The celebration would last several days. As honoured guests we must make the rounds of all the families. We should have the strength and determination for a celebration of, perhaps, a week of food and booze with short naps between gluts.

It was getting dark. We thanked our hosts, again and again, and asked to leave, explaining over and over that we had a date early next morning with the mighty Wanganui. No way, Jake! The Maoris would have nothing of this. Some of the guests, suffering no doubt from the affects of the heat, alcohol and the season's goodwill were getting belligerent. In the night, when the party slackened off and a general drowsiness overcame the crowd, we silently slunk away to our rendezvous on the riverbank. A drunken, but no doubt joking, mention of *long-pig* added speed to our flight.

The first two days on the Wanganui were delightful: rapids around every corner, magnificent scenery, warm sun, good companions. On the morning of the third day all that changed. The scream of a Long-tailed Cuckoo broke the pre-dawn silence, then a most unusual bird song like the tinkling of a silver bell (I have never heard a silver bell tinkling but this was what it must sound like) announced the arrival of a new day. Another and then another joined the serenade. There were three notes beginning high, and the birds seemed to be singing in concert. I could imagine a small feathered conductor waving his baton way up there on the tallest rata. Against the silent background of primeval forest, in the grey light of receding night the music had a melancholy effect. It lasted only a few minutes before other birds, Blackbirds, Dunnocks and Song Thrushes, all assisted immigrants from England, took over. We looked out. The sky was a cheerless solid grey. From the shrouding forest, curtains of vapour rose into the aerial reservoir that was about to spill over. Yes, the first drops splashed down, a prelude to a major incoming weather front. Over a damp breakfast, a local weather wizard mumbled, "I think we can expect heavy precipitation."

He was right. The rest of the river trip was wet above, below and sideways. Negotiating one of the many rapids, we skimmed up on a barely water-covered flat rock. The current threatened to capsize us, so Peter and I jumped overboard to steady the dinghy and push it off. Fortunately, the water was only a bit more than waist deep, but unfortunately, our life raft had been butchered by a knife-edge projection just an inch below the water. We were in no danger of sinking as the tube containing the air was intact, but there was a gash in the floor. We were now sitting right on the waterline, the dinghy hardly visible. Most of our supplies were secure in watertight bags but not all. Sometime later we noticed the water in the boat looked like porridge and there was a tail of gruel seeping out behind us. The Creamota sack had burst. There went breakfast. The cheese, the size and thickness of an ancient grind-stone, fared well, for it was case-hardened and indestructible. The cheese had been responsible for the mishap as its weight caused the rubber floor to sag just enough to catch the sharp rock.

The next day our supply load was dried figs, McIntosh toffees, canned corned beef and two cases of Eno's fruit salts. Our victualler had ordered the fruit salts in the belief that the chemicals would counteract the starch-cheese diet and lack of exercise. Another theory was the salts could be a purifying agent for the Wanganui water. But nature can screw up the best laid plans and theories. The river water was carrying a load

Ruth and Margaret launching the dinghy.

of waste from the interminable herds of sheep and cows grazing on the grassy hills above. Only two days on the river and everyone was heading for the bushes clutching soggy bits of note paper or a handful of rough fern leaves. We hadn't heard of e-coli in those days. We had *the Wanganui fox-trots*. A fierce epidemic of explosive dysentery or something so close one couldn't tell the difference had struck and continued spasmodically until journey's end. Our quartermaster had goofed. A recipe for discomfort: Wanganui water, two cases of Eno's Salts but no toilet paper.

That night we slept in a shearing shed after an almost impossible, slippery climb up a mud cliff. The shed was dry but a thousand sheep had recently left their mark. When we were tucked in dry in our sleeping bags, the roar of the rain on the tin roof gave us the comforting feeling that the abundant sheep turds were really only wild grapes.

Disaster struck again on the oatmeal-cheese day. Our floating home developed a slow air leak. A long day in a rubber dinghy is uncomfortable anytime but on half inflation it is godawfull. Aches developed in every muscle and fanned out to congeal in an acme of pain. There was no relief because of the sagging feather-bed effect of our craft. Manoeuvrability, not great at any time, was reduced to zero. There was a pump in another dinghy somewhere along the river. It had to be there because we didn't have it. We drifted into an eddy, hanging back. We thought dinghy number two was somewhere behind us. While we waited we heard loud caterwauling reverberating from the canyon walls. Then a canoe, barely afloat, with two voyageurs, appeared. Only the fore and aft ends of the canoe were above water. Two men sitting up to their life jackets in the same liquid were paddling furiously and singing, "*In the Blue Canadian Rockies.*" Even in our state of numbness it was a hilarious scene. We were partly submerged but safe on an underwater rock when around the bend our rescuers appeared. They had the pump. Soon the rubber ring was swollen and we pushed off into swift water. More trouble; the bung blew out! Over inflation. Now we did have a problem. We were in mid-river, up the creek, but with paddles this time. Sheer dripping banks on both sides. We dug in our paddles. Peter had his thumb in the bung hole slowing the exit of air. We pushed for a ledge that miraculously jutted out from the black face. We piled up on the finest little rock table I had ever seen. Perhaps the Wanganui River goddess, looking up from her slimy home, decided to give us another chance; perhaps she was just having some fun.

Long after dark, wet and chilled, we and most of our companions trickled in to a roaring bonfire and welcome accommodation in an old Maori meeting house well above the river. We were delighted to thaw out and to have dry beds. Our feet and butts had that corrugated feel of *washerwoman's hands*. Others were not so fortunate. A couple decided to camp on a ledge near the river instead of attempting the treacherous climb in the darkness up the mud cliff. A midnight downpour collapsed their tent and soaked their sleeping bags. In the morning they staggered in, more dead than alive.

On the Wanganui River.

We didn't see many animals on the trip and any seen were promptly shot. Other than a couple of bat species there were no mammals in New Zealand prior to the coming of the Maoris and later, the Europeans. With the Europeans came a veritable zoo of exotic species both domestic and wild. Lacking natural predators, goats of several kinds and Red Deer were knocking supreme hell out of the vegetation. Perhaps the most famous of the assisted mammal immigrants is the *Captain Cooker*: a powerful, hairy wild boar introduced to the islands by Captain Cook in order to give the natives a good source of protein and to steer them away from cannibalism. Domestic pigs have taken to the hills since Cook's time, diluting the original stock. Today many wild pigs are indistinguishable from the tame variety. A true *Cooker*, with massive head and front

CANADIAN VISITORS

MOTOR-CYCLE TOUR.

Mr and Mrs D. Stirling, of Canada, have set out on what they expect to be a two-year tour of the world by motor-cycle. So far, they have only got as far as Palmerston North, but time is no object to this carefree couple.

Brought up in Athabasca, Alberta, Mr Stirling has been working in Victoria, British Columbia, for the last two years, first as a fisheries inspector for the Government and later as an electrician in a shi yard.

Mr and Mrs Stirling first took bus to San Francisco where they joined the Orion and arrived in Auckland on May 14. They worked around Auckland for five months and then in the first week of November set off on their tour.

Two other Canadians, Mr and Mrs P. Duval, who have been working in Palmerston North, are also travelling by motor-cycle through New Zealand.

They plan to leave here on Monday for Taumarunui to join the Auckland Canoe Club's Wanganui River trip. The party leaves Taumarunui on Boxing Day in rubber dinghies (for the "tenderfoot") and canoes. So far 60 have booked in for the journey which is expected to take 10 days.

New Year's Eve will be spent in Pipiriki where a party and dance has been arranged.

Mr and Mrs Stirling will then return to Palmerston North for the rest of their gear and then head southwards to Wellington and the South Island.

After that they will probably spend some time in Australia. "Our plans are a bit vague at present," was Mr Stirling's comment.

DOWN RIVER TRIP

CANADIANS RETURN.

RAIN SPOILS VOYAGE.

Down the Wanganui River with the Auckland Canoe Club's party between Christmas and New Year was a worthwhile experience for the Canadian couple, Mr and Mrs D. Stirling, who have returned to the city motor camp after making the trip.

The couple travelled on the river with another Canadian pair, Mr and Mrs P. Duval, who have also come back to the city. Mrs Stirling summed the experience up with enthusiastic praise for the scenery. The only thing which went wrong was the weather. It rained and rained most of the time, a contributing factor which made the Canadians decide to pull out on New Year's Day at Pipiriki instead of carrying on

Mrs Stirling would have liked a few photographs of the river on the way down from Taumarunui, but with so much rain the cameras were wrapped up securely and it was not worth getting them out.

When the bad weather persisted it was decided to spend a day in a shearing shed. "It had been used quite recently by sheep, but it was so wet we were glad to see that shearing shed."

This day also provided a respite from tinned meals. Some of the party were upset by this type of food. All there was to do was just float along and eat," said Mrs Stirling.

The best day saw the various crafts cover 30 miles, but it needed a fair amount of paddling to get as far as that. The Canadian couples were together in a rubber dinghy. On one occasion the valve slipped and the dinghy quickly deflated when the craft was on a stretch of water from which high banks sheered up on both sides. One solitary ledge at just the right place enabled the dinghy to be landed in the nick of time.

And still the rain kept on, so the Canadians, having seen what was described as the best part of the river, had had enough. After all, for most New Zealand campers such a trip is an annual holiday, but when all the equipment in the dinghy is your "house" it is worth looking after. Besides, light raincoats were badly tattered and the rain was still coming down.

From the
MANAWATU STANDARD
Dec 22 & ??, 1956

quarters, long legs and a black, hairy razor back, is a formidable beast. The pigs and their families with their tough, but sensitive snouts are blamed for much carnage among the native plants.

Early in the trip someone bagged a young goat. The meat was parceled out at tea time. The same day, one of the club's officers knocked over a magnificent Captain Cooker. The carcass was hung by the heels for all to admire. It wasn't eaten. It was pronounced *wormy* and was probably as tough as an old horse with its harness on. Still, it seemed a shame to shoot this noble beast in the first place and to leave it for the bluebottles. Once we saw a young goat standing on a tall boulder completely cut off by the rising river. The kid looked our way and bleated, perhaps hoping for rescue. Two men in a canoe swept around the corner. The crash of a .303 rifle filled the canyon. Another carcass to feed the eels. The piteous cries of the goat and the crash of the gunshot echoed over and over again. These sounds last only a moment; the murmuring and gurgling of the Wanganui will go on for another million years.

Speaking of eels; in New Zealand they grow big. How big? We heard many tales of great eels *as thick as a man's body; ten feet long; bent the tines of the pitchfork when I speared it; if Jonah had lived in New Zealand he would have been swallowed by an eel.* No doubt there is a bit of piscatorial exaggeration in these stories, but we did see several big black specimens that would rival two lengths of the six-inch thick stove pipe that was connected to the airtight wood stove on the old homestead. Near Golden Bay on the northwest corner of the South Island, a woman had been feeding eels for umpteen years. Gentle, big fellows of fourteen pounds ate hamburger from her hand and lay patiently for a tickle under the chin. Perhaps eels, like most other animals, need only a little T.L.C.

In New Zealand, as elsewhere in the world, people considered eels either a delicacy or an abomination. In the Australian outback we met a homesick Cockney who reminisced, almost tearfully, about jellied eels in parsley sauce. On the other hand, eels are slimy. *Slimy* is really off-putting. It is often used to describe a politician. Eels resemble snakes (another term for an unloved person); a good excuse to bar them from the dinner plate. The eel's tenacity for life is proverbial; it doesn't stop twitching until digested – a put-off for all but the most unfeeling gourmet.

Fishing for eels was a favourite activity on the Wanganui. With torch and a bit of meat on a hook, eels were pulled out with astonishing rapidity. They would even snap on to a piece of white rag on a string and hang tight until grounded. Another method of decimating the slimy animal's population is to toss the entrails of a luckless rabbit, pig or whatever into the stream and stand by with torch and spear.

Our flotation device successfully negotiated the last two major rapids on the river and deposited us at our destination, Pipiriki, a backcountry sheep town. Since it was New Year's Eve we had a booze-up and dance at the local *Palaise de Dance* where a Maori band entertained us with their rendition of *Po Kari Kari Anna* and *Mambo Rock*.

Next day we had to get back to Palmerton North where our bikes were waiting. We begged a lift with a wealthy resident who, with his large empty station wagon, was the only person going out that day. He charged us two pounds each for the thirty-mile ride. We were so astonished we paid him. Two pounds was a fortune for us at that time. Fortunately, his kind is a rarity in New Zealand.

5

BIRDING ALONG THE CONWAY

Wellington was wet and windy as Wellington is supposed to be, but the Pohutukawa trees were in full lovely red bloom. Our bike, with all our possessions, was hoisted aboard the South Island ferry by a sling. It looked very disastrous, but it hit the deck in one piece. We boarded damp and bedraggled. Out in the Cook Strait the sun burst through the prevailing overcast. We sat in a sunny spot and dried out while watching Southern black- backed Gulls, Giant Petrels and our first Wandering Albatross escort the ferry across the blue water. Soon, far off to the south, the snow capped-peaks of the Kaikouras broached the horizon.

The eastern part of the South Island was a different country. Here the grass was brown, the countryside dry, not at all like the verdant hills of the North we left behind. Once ashore we stretched out on the dry earth and ate our lunch while enjoying the trilling of the crickets.

We met Peter and Margaret again in Wellington after having gone our separate ways after the Wanganui trip. We travelled together again south as far as Christchurch. On the rugged east coast where the view alternates between enormous expanses of distant green mountains and enormous expanses of blue Pacific, Peter's bike packed it in. Carrying out engine first aid we found a broken piston ring. After an executive meeting the girls volunteered to hitchhike into Christchurch for the necessary parts while the boys made camp and stripped the machine. The breakdown had occurred at a propitious location. A quick *recce* found a sheep station tucked away in a magnificent grove of Monterey Pines. We asked the *cocky* (New Zealand farmer) for permission to camp under his trees. The cocky insisted we move into the comfort of the shearers' huts and as a bonus said, "Help yourselves to the plums." The homestead was overgrown with plum trees of several varieties, their branches breaking with fruit. Since fruit had been a lean item in our diet we feasted.

Next morning Peter went to the river to tempt the trout; I opted for birding. The Conway, like most rivers on the South Island, flows through a wide braided valley of stones. In flood times the river spreads out into numerous and shifting channels; in summer the river is reduced to a number of shallow streams meandering hither and yon through a wilderness of shingle. Plants can only gain a foothold on areas safe from high water for several seasons. Chief among the pioneer plants is the exotic yellow lupine: tall as a man, blowing in clumps over this strange landscape. Purple mountains on the distant western horizon, sunlight shimmering on the grey shingle, milky glacial water tinkling down to the sea, forests of lupines and lots of new birds. What a morning!

Delicate Black-fronted Terns patrolled the watercourses, Pied Oystercatchers, Pied Stilts and Banded Dotterels were everywhere. I saw bold kingfishers and timid New Zealand Pipits. Around a river bend I surprised a White-faced Heron, a patient fisherman, out for a late breakfast. Perhaps the most beautiful of all the morning's birds was the Paradise Duck. I watched a family, mum with striking white head and neck; dad, rich chocolate brown with white wing flashes, and two brown children. If the Paradise Duck took the beauty prize, the Wrybill, a small plover with a curved beak, not up as in avocet nor down as in curlew but sideways for picking up bugs around corners, was the strangest. It seems that most, if not all, Wrybills are *right billed*. Its inconspicuous colour, mostly grey above and white below, makes it look like just another stone among millions. Wrybills nest among the stones of these South Island rivers and spend the winter on the broad estuaries of the North Island.

Predators and scavengers, Australian Harriers and gulls, were enjoying the good life, as this was the season when a new crop of young birds was introduced into the river environment. I found only two foreign bird species: the Skylark, dominant bird of the open land, and the aggressive Australian Magpie. Magpies, when tired of harassing other birds, were carolling melodiously from the tree tops. While birding the Conway River, my thoughts strayed back to birding along the original Conway in North Wales thirteen years previously.

Our idyll beside the Conway was soon over. The girls returned with the spare parts, the bike was fixed and we were on the road again down the Canterbury Plains. The country, mostly dry grass, looked like the Canadian Prairies except that broad belts of pine and eucalyptus trees soon dispelled that resemblance. We stopped briefly in Christchurch, city of the plain, founded by Canterbury pilgrims who planned an English cathedral city in the distant new lands of the Antipodes. The streets are named after Anglican bishoprics, the cathedral and ivy-covered colleges are a bit of old England. After sightseeing we pushed on south to Timaru, Omaru and Dunedin. Christchurch is old England; Dunedin is new Scotland. Founded by Scottish Presbyterian immigrants, Dunedin is known as the Edinburgh of the South. From the highway just north of the city the panoramic view of Otago Harbour is superb.

We rode through central Otago to Roxburgh and beyond over a barren plateau littered with strange geological monuments: piles of horizontal weathered strata like sheets of mica. The only signs of life were Skylarks and harriers. Along the Clutha River cherries and peaches were ripe. Roadside stands were mountains of fruit. We made frequent stops.

Queenstown, on Lake Wakatipu, under the wall of the Remarkables, was a scenic place to exercise our numb backsides after the long, slow ride from Glen Colwyn sheep station on the Conway River. Queenstown is a favourite tourist resort and headquarters for trips to the mountain and lake country that stretches from Mt. Cook to Milford Sound. Sheep stations encompassing thousands of acres are located here. The original fern and scrub vegetation has been replaced with grass to nourish a million hungry woollies. At Queenstown we met Vic and Betty Macdonald, another Canadian couple, now managing a tourist camp in the vicinity. We had met them briefly on the *Orion*. It's a small world, indeed. We spent some time together fishing and exploring the country.

Queenstown is just a shade off forty-five degrees south latitude, half way between the equator and the South Pole. We had reason to believe the Antarctic was even closer when a powerful storm terminated the glorious summer weather. The river of maritime polar air behind the front sent us shivering into our tent. Next morning there was snow on Ben Nevis. It was more like midwinter than midsummer when we left for Te Anau.

The thirty-mile stretch between Lumsden and Te Anau was under construction. Even a preacher on a bike would have polluted the air with blasphemy. Keeping upright in the deep, coarse road-metal was a proper bastard. A swarm of monster construction machines forced us out onto the verges. Showers of missiles bounced off our jackets and goggles, and a strong, cold southerly headwind roused up acres of dust and retarded our progress. Sharp bits of road foundation picked up by the front wheel and fired back with deadly accuracy brought howls of pain when they contacted our legs. My numb hands still had a death grip on the steering bars at journey's end.

We arrived at the AA camp with visions of hot showers and a good stretch, but this was not in the cards, for non-members had to fork up twelve shillings for a spot even for a pup tent and a motorcycle. Twelve shillings, not much you say? Well, we had to watch our money as we had only six pounds between us and finding work again. Checking around, we found a beautiful secluded campsite by the Eglinton River with plenty of dry beech wood. No hot showers but absolute privacy, great scenery and a hot campfire and all free!

Next day we continued our travels. Off in the distance the dark Murchison Mountains, home to the Takahea, a twenty-inch-tall, six-pound, iridescent blue, flightless member of the rail family. A vegetarian, it shears off succulent basal shoots of the tussock grass. The first known specimen was eaten by some hungry whalers in Dusky Sound in 1849. It was thought to be extinct until a small colony was discovered in the Murchison wilderness in 1948. The government declared a large chunk of its range a preserve, out of bounds to all except *bona fide* ornithologists. [Takaheas have been introduced elsewhere. The public can see them now on Tiritiri Island near Auckland.]

The Eglinton Valley scenery was magnificent but the weather was an absolute failure. The temperature got colder, the wind windier, the rain wetter. We arrived in Cascade Creek in a near-perished condition. On a grassy flat near the river we set up our wet tent on a stray sheet of corrugated iron in order to keep us from sinking into the bog. We got a magnificent bonfire raging, brewed up a billy of hot tea and crawled into our sleeping bags. We used the massive Sunday newspaper bought in Queenstown to cover our sleeping bags to help absorb the fine mist penetrating the tent roof as we didn't have a fly. An hour later, snug, secure and warm we listened to the battering of the rain and the roar of the wind. The contrast, separated only by a thin piece of cotton and a sheet of corrugated iron, was wonderful. Life was good.

Awake early next morning (can you sleep late on a sheet of corrugated iron?) we found no cheer in God's great outdoors. (No, we were not trying to prove some silly personal thing by suffering. We enjoyed nature's moods, well, most of the time. Now we were impecunious and frugal.) Through breaks in the mist we saw fresh snow on the mountains. We brewed up and ate a stand-up breakfast of bread and tea. There was no dry place to sit. We were ankle deep in moss and water. While contemplating the gloomy scene we reviewed our financial situation. In a minute we came to the conclusion that our net worth was just a shade above zero. Early employment was indicated. But where was work? There were quick, casual jobs in the Nelson country at the top end of the Island where farmers were crying out for fruit pickers. We would have to reverse north but first we wanted to see Milford Sound, regardless of bad weather and lack of money. We squelched over to the little store for a can of bully beef. In conversation with the proprietor we told him we were hoping for a break in the weather before continuing to Milford Sound.

"I can get you a dry ride about noon," he said. "Why not leave your bike and gear here and catch one of the empty buses going in to pick up a party of hikers?" A fine idea!

Later that afternoon we were rolling in comfort through the Homer Tunnel and down the road that drops three thousand feet to sea level at the Sound. During breaks in the clouds we saw snowy peaks, lush forest and sheer granite slopes, the world-famous scenery of Milford Sound. Waterfalls and cascades were exploding everywhere.

The scenery was overpowering but we had to think about a bed under a dry roof and several bouts of eating before we got back to our tent. The Milford Hotel was beyond our purse but we were forced to splurge for bed and breakfast at three guineas for two at the AA cabins. What luxury to have a warm cabin, a dry bed and a refuge from the hordes of black flies. Black flies are the only biting insect pest in New Zealand. You can find them everywhere, but they are a terror only on the rainy west coast.

The next morning after more awesome gazing (in New Zealand we did a lot of awesome gazing as you might have noticed) we caught a ride back to Cascade Creek with an amiable cow cocky. That evening we made our home in a sequestered tea tree grove beside beautiful Lake Manapouri. Weather today: sunny and warm.

The Bellbirds were staging a pre-dawn concert. This time it was not the melancholy tones of the Wanganui; this time it was like the tinkling of a battery of musical powder boxes. It was difficult to believe that birds were making this music. Perhaps there was an organ grinder standing beside our tent directing the musicians. It was the beginning of a glorious day in this mountain solitude.

Although our sojourn in the south had been vexed with some *crook* weather, we had been amply rewarded with sightings of new birds. We first met the South Island Robin, fearless sprite of the forest, along the Eglinton Valley. This small bird inhabiting the ground and low shrubbery is absolutely fearless, not a good attitude for survival. Robins followed us in the forest, attracted to insects stirred up by our boots. They even landed on our heads and hands. With our robin escort we saw Yellow-fronted Parakeets, Yellow Heads and tiny Riflemen. Large parrots with white heads, Kakas, most widely-distributed of New Zealand's three big parrots, flew screaming to their feeding trees. Another large parrot, the Kea, noted for its mischievous antics, gained a reputation in earlier times as a sheep killer. A sheep-killing parrot? The Kea has a massive hooked beak ideal for extracting bulbs and roots. Perhaps one hard winter a Kea, checking out a sheep carcass tasted kidney fat and found it good. Kea onlookers took up the habit. The next step was tallow on the hoof. Living sheep were accessible and even more plentiful. Not all Keas were sheep killers, but who can tell the difference. Bountied, hundreds fell to instant lead poisoning. Now, Keas are confined to the mountains where they charm tourists with their amusing antics and satisfy their destructive urges by vandalizing car windshield wipers and hikers' backpacks. The third New Zealand parrot is the Kakapo, a sap-green owl-faced bird about two feet long. Flightless, it feeds on the tender basal stems of tussock grass. A recovery plan is in place to save this rare species from extinction.

Bellbirds, Tuis, Fantails and Grey Warblers were common. We saw hawk-like Long-tailed Cuckoos and smaller Shining Cuckoos, both brood parasites, summer visitors to New Zealand from their winter homes in the Melanesian Islands. European imports were much in evidence almost everywhere – House Sparrows, Yellowhammers, Redpolls, Song Thrushes and Blackbirds – except in the deepest forests where native birds were still supreme.

Walking was difficult in these forests as giant moss-covered fallen trees barred the way. Evergreen beech trees up to five feet in diameter and towering to over a hundred feet in height formed sombre forests on the ocean side of the Southern Alps. Other tree species and shrubs were scarce, only mosses and lichens of fantastic shape and colour covered fallen wood and living branches.

Riding north again we camped beyond Porter's Pass west of Christchurch. All around were silent, desiccated mountains for we were in the rain shadow of the main ranges. From our camp a dry beech forest extended down the valley. The trees were smaller but it was a silent world, a natural monoculture of beech trees, weird lichens and parasitic mistletoes. The subdued voices of tiny, sombre plumaged birds, such as Brown Creepers or Pipipi and Riflemen, only intensified the feeling of solitude. Here was, indeed, the outermost part of the Earth.

Out in the sunlight on the seemingly barren slopes we found a variety of plants of the woolly, hairy and succulent species, adapted to survive in a hostile environment. Long-eared European hares bounded over the slopes. These animals, together with the insatiable appetites of domestic sheep and feral goats, are contributing to the demise of many native plants.

We were camped in a calm spot where only a rare puff of wind stirred our tent, but at intervals we could hear a swishing roar coming up from below that at its height filled the whole valley with sound before dying away in the sky. Then, dead silence again before the next wave. It was *the roar of the mountain*, a tsunami of sound, a phenomenon caused by gale-force wind rushing through a mountain pass. From a hill-top we could see, far down the pass, the beech forest flattening and twisting in huge waves before the wind. The uncanny roar was the soughing of a million trees in a natural wind tunnel.

We took the Otiro Gorge route, which roughly parallels the five-and-a-half-mile railway tunnel through the mountains, to the west coast. The road was a series of hairpin bends roughly connected by deep loose gravel: a biker's nightmare. The descent was so steep we ran in low gear with throttle closed and brakes on. What a relief to arrive down on the west coast physically in one piece but mentally wiped out. From Greymouth to Westport the scenery was spectacular. Huge rollers sweeping in from the Tasman Sea, mountain vistas, dense forests, golden sands, sea caves and pancake rocks. New Zealand is a land of spectacular scenery from one end to the other.

6

NICOTINE SUMMER

We arrived at a well-appointed campground in Nelson, capital of the *Garden of the South*. This sunny, fertile country was a cornucopia of orchards, gardens, hop fields and tobacco plantations. In these hot summer days, stridulating cicadas with three-inch wing spans seemed to vibrate the air.

While searching for a choice campsite beneath the *Radiata* pines we noticed two tents that looked familiar. Yes, it was the wandering Canadian bikers, Peter and Margaret and Vic and Betty. Peter and Margaret had arrived last night; Vic and Betty had just hauled in. Although having different agendas and travelling by different routes, three couples had arrived in Nelson within a twelve-hour period. I won't repeat that small-world cliché again, but it was on my mind.

After a suitable reunion of tea and the recapitulation of recent adventures we decided that high-paying temporary employment was necessary. There was a paucity of fruit pickers. After speaking to some potential employers we found ourselves in a new role. We are tobacco harvesters on K.J.'s plantation of beautiful Golden Virginia plants stretching in neat five-foot-tall rows towards the distant mountains. Tobacco, America's gift to mankind, was a major commercial crop. Hardening the lungs with smoke from a tube of smouldering leaves is popular the world over.

A tobacco worker's job description: a strong back and nimble fingers. There is a division of labour according to sex. Men pick the leaves starting at the ripe bottom *lugs* of each plant and work up as ripening progresses with the season. Harvesting takes about six weeks, as two or three leaves are plucked at each picking. Crouching, the picker waddles along the row, snapping off leaves with thumb and forefinger and transferring them to the growing bundle between arm number two and adjacent side of body. As the season moves on, the worker straightens up a few inches each day until at the end of the harvest he is standing tall again. Unless he is permanently crippled. At row's end the leaves are dumped on a rack. The racks are then hauled to the kiln where the women's work begins. A day's labour is a full kiln. Men's work is hot and back-breaking; women's is quick and tedious, mitigated somewhat by singing, jokes and gossip. Women are *passing* and *tying*. The passer picks up two or three golden leaves and hands them to the tyer who with a couple of half hitches arranges the bunches neatly along a four-foot tea-tree pole. Speed is the keynote here. The title of *gun tyer* is the ambition of many novices. Tobacco tying competitions were a feature of farm fairs in the Nelson country.

The sticks, adorned with tobacco leaves, are hung to cure in a kiln which looks like a sawed-off replica of a Canadian prairie grain elevator. Even heat from a furnace, together with the variety of tobacco plant and

Women at work: passing and tying.

height of the leaf on the stem, will determine the quality of the finished product.

The first week in the nicotine patch was easy. We were *lateralling*, picking off buds that grow from the leaf bracts. Nature intended the tobacco plant to be a bush-shaped affair but we have other ideas. We want large leaves on one tall stem without side shoots. We were walking straight up along the rows, enjoying the clean warm air of late summer. That was about to change.

One morning we were initiated into reality. We had to fill a kiln with *lugs*. Since these little ground-huggers were only a fraction of the size of normal leaves it will take a huge quantity to fill a kiln. Even worse, it was going to be hot and we were waddling down the rows plucking, with our noses just above the earth – the lowest crouch possible. Any lower we would have been making furrows in the dirt. Add all this to the fact that we were months free from manual labour and you had, come sundown, three totally knackered males.

A tobacco girl proud of her handiwork.

What a day! From 7:00 a.m. to 6:00 p.m. we laboured in the fields of yellow tobacco. Now, stretched out on a grassy knoll, nursing the pain of known and unknown muscles creeping back to their usual places, we were grateful when K.J. arrived with beer bottles, one, two, three. Surveying the rigid, dirty, nicotine-encrusted, sweaty bodies he said, "Good work, lads, have a cool beer."

We had just enough strength left to lift one and suck it down without a pause. It was the brew of paradise. K.J. began a monologue: In a week we will be in superb condition, tough, bronzed, and happy as Captain Cookers. We will even enjoy the healthy outdoor work, and so on and so forth. We were too exhausted to reply.

That night we talked. Two couples decided to go for other less backbreaking work. We decided to stay. Being of a scientific turn of mind, I decided to stick it out for another week just to test K.J.'s theory.

I staggered through that week in a painful daze but come the Sabbath I knew I had become at least as tough as a dead Captain Cooker. I tried one more week. K.J. was right. Like Kipling's Gunga Din, *"the unicorn [or was it* uniform, *although unicorn would be much more spectacular] he wore, it wasn't much before and rather less than half of that behind"*, I was romping down the rows topless, in straw hat, ragged short shorts and bare feet with an underarm load of green leaves leaking brown sap. The juice combined with sweat and dust formed a crust that covers most of the body from fingertips via arm pits to belly button. The crust came off with soap, hot water and scrubbing but the stain lingered for weeks. The next five weeks were among the most enjoyable days we spent in New Zealand.

There were some rare characters amongst the itinerant workers in the Motueka Valley. The weekend nightlife was robust. Much to the annoyance of the farmers who are anxious to see fruit off the trees and tobacco in the kilns, monumental Saturday night *plonk* (cheap wine) and barbecue parties flared up down by the river, often still raging on Monday morning when trees and fields beckoned to be harvested. On the bright side, there was no better place than God's outdoors for a tobacco pickers' ball. Destruction of property by beery battlers and excited hula dancers was, like frost and hail, just one of the many headaches confronting growers at harvest time.

Bert, a wiry little chap, deserves honourable mention. Bert's sole reason for breathing was the pursuit of happiness – beer, plonk and women. He was the life of Saturday night's booze-up, but on Monday morning an old complaint, *sand on the stomach*, contracted during his war days in Egypt, recurred. Late in the afternoon Bert surfaced. Sand on the stomach had been flushed out thanks to a couple of bottles of Dominion lager, and by sundown he was giving us a continuous commentary, in non-technical language, of his drinking and amorous adventures. Saturday saw him off again to worship Bacchus and Aphrodite. In all fairness it must be said that Bert was a hard worker between parties, although he said he was here only for the social life. He was a dedicated man.

Near midnight there was a loud rap on our door. Allan burst in, in a state of fear and excitement. Mary, one of the tobacco workers, was being bashed around by her ex-husband who had appeared from nowhere, drunk as a hoot owl. I was needed to help rescue Mary. We rushed to the cabins where some of the workers were billeted. Outside, Mary and her ex, a massive Maori, were arguing. Ex delivered a couple of head busting slaps to Mary's face. I stepped forward and said something like, "Stop it."

The giant stretched out a paw the size of a twenty-dollar smoked ham and attached it to my shirt collar. "Yank," he said [I didn't think it was either the time or the place to inform him that by birth and passport I am a Canadian, nor did I shout loud and clear, *I am Canadian!* like the guy in a recent Molson's beer TV commercial]. "Yank," he said, "You are a married man. You must know you don't get involved in someone else's domestic quarrel."

His short lecture was very convincing especially since my toes were reaching out for the ground. At that moment little Bert appeared with a tea-tree stick long as a broom handle and as hard as iron. He bent the shillelagh around the giant's rib cage with a thump that would drop an ox. The big man seemed to be immune to pain, but he released my neck from his paw and as Bert gathered momentum for another blow he grabbed the stick, fired it away, seized his attacker, swung him around overhead and hurled him into the tobacco patch. Fortunately during the donnybrook Mary ran off to the safety of the boss's house. The giant staggered away into the night. Bert rose up from the herbage, still fighting mad, shouting, "If that bastard comes here again I'll have his balls bronzed for bookends."

I couldn't imagine Bert with a book. He certainly had courage or a skinful or both. In WW II, he must have been a terror to Rommel's Afrika Korps.

We had some strange pets during our stay amongst the Golden Virginia. Knowing of our interest in nature, Francis, a tobacco girl, and the boys presented us with any homeless creature they discovered. Naturalists are supposed to be willing and able to look after all animal flotsam. One of these was a pale green two-inch praying mantis that lived happily around the windowsill and on the ceiling until the night it snuggled into my sleeping bag, giving me one hellofa fright. Mabel, the mantis, was unceremoniously hurled out the window, fortunately open at that time. Then there was a five-inch-long stick insect which, although of formidable appearance, was just a harmless vegetarian. A foul-smelling black cockroach or Maori bug was returned to the great outdoors right after day one. A sullen, large and hairy trap-door spider lived with us until we moved on. We admired her silken tunnel complete with a cunningly-hinged circular lid.

One dark evening we were summoned out onto the veranda where Allan stood proudly beside a heap of dead possums. Possums, assisted immigrants from Australia, reproducing like rabbits, were converting the island's vegetation to pellets and generally being a nuisance. A bounty of two shilling had been placed on their heads. Australian possums, unlike American opossums, have thickly furred tails with just a short naked prehensile area underneath. Their coats range from greyish through rufous and amber to almost black. Their pelts made *coonskin* hats during the Davy Crocket craze. The call of the possum is a low laugh, hoarse and mad, guaranteed to raise goose pimples and the hair on the neck of the tenderfoot bush walker.

One of the deceased animals was a mother with a live baby in her pouch. Allan handed the baby to Ruth. It is a hairless mite not particularly beautiful. It lived only a week on a diet of cow's milk and glucose.

Peter the rabbit, whose ancestors had come from England, was the friendliest pet of the lot. We rescued Peter and brother Bugs (not original names) from the farm dog that was happily digging out a burrow in the tobacco field. Francis took Bugs and Ruth took Peter. Peter's clan, multiplying like rabbits, had become serious pests to both wild and domestic vegetation. The government was waging a war of rabbit genocide. In fact keeping a pet rabbit was illegal at that time. Our rabbit lived in a vacant room piled high with bolts of cloth used for covering delicate young tobacco plants in the spring. In the cloth mountains, bunny had many lairs and observation posts.

We hiked up the track leading to Mt. Arthur one sunny autumn morning. With us were fellow tobacco workers Francis, Allan and Paul – all, except us, heavily armed. Sheep grazed in the bracken growing among the charred stumps of bygone forest trees. Flocks of Goldfinches, Redpolls and Chaffinches fed on the clumps of tall thistles, mullein and foxgloves. From boulder lookouts sentinel California Quail called loudly "Tobacco, tobacco!"

A pleasant scene for eye and ear but this was not *old* New Zealand. We paused to seek out nature past. Below, along the creek, there was a thin remnant of matai, rimu and beech with an understorey of palm-like tree ferns; on a distant ridge rata flaunted its crimson blossoms against a polished blue sky. Our eyes spied several Pied Fantails dancing about like shuttlecocks; our ears picked up the distant tickling and belling of Tuis and Bellbirds. A flock of Silvereyes fed with the abundant immigrant finches. As the day warmed, the air crackled with the stridulations of a thousand cicadas. It was a glorious morning in the Southern Hemisphere. Yes, remnants of old nature were still here but they were being submerged.

The sun rose higher and so did the elevation. Sweat glistened on our foreheads and soaked our shirts as we humped our bodies and packsacks over the rough terrain. By a cool mossy spring in the shade of the silent beech forest we dropped our loads and stretched out for a short breather. The primeval silence was broken by the uncanny cries of a Weka, a chicken-sized flightless rail, now becoming rare. While introduced goats and deer demolish the vegetation, stoats, rats and feral cats have a field day among the tame and flightless birds that never before had to deal with four-legged hairy predators.

Next stop was Flora Hut, one of these corrugated iron affairs that are like ovens in the sunshine and like the polar ice cap after dark. While brewing up we found an unusual snail on the floor. It was about two-and-a-half inches in diameter, spirally banded, lined with reddish brown on a yellowish background. This was one of the curious and carnivorous Kauri Snails of which thirty-eight species inhabit New Zealand. The one we were admiring was *Paryphonta hochstetteri*.

We had a lazy afternoon sun bathing, reading and taking short walks in the sombre woods where the silence was only occasionally interrupt-ed by calls of Tuis and Kakas. We could only imagine that cities choked with people existed anywhere on Earth. For lovers of solitude we recom-mend the hoary beech forests of New Zealand's Alps.

We were on the trail early next morning, after a bitterly cold night. The crackling of dry leaves indicated the approach of something big. It was a chunky billy goat that had the misfortune to be out on his daily stroll. The mountain silence was shattered by the crash of Allan's .303 rifle, and then Paul's rifle blazed. The unlucky beast lay dying with hid-eous wounds, bleating piteously as its life blood flowed away. The tail was hacked off for the three-shilling government bounty; the carcass was left for the big bold blue-tailed flies.

Bluebottles deserve mention as they were exceedingly abundant and formidable pests. This blowfly with black thorax and violet blue abdo-men is about a half inch in length. It not only *blows* meat but also the wool on the sheep and even woollen clothing hanging out in the sun-light. But they do fit in to nature's organization. In a country where most wild animals are serious environmental pests, possums, rabbits, goats and deer die in thousands from trapping, hunting and poison baits. In re-mote mountains, goats and deer were slaughtered by government hunt-ers. The carcasses were left to rot, as packing out was difficult and there was a glut of domestic meat on the market anyway. In the mountains, since there are neither carrion birds in the air nor scavenging mammals on the ground, the bluebottle rules in the domain of dead flesh.

After the goat episode we had a brief but steep climb to a new world. Trees, short and contorted, seemed to be smothering under a heavy blanket of mosses and lichens. Beech trees were dominant but there were some quaint screw pines and loose-barked cedars. Except for dead leaves, the ground carpet of lichens and mosses was devoid of other plants. Twisted white dead branches and long filaments of grey-beard lichens added to the atmosphere of endless hoary age. Outside of the vegetable kingdom, the only sign of life was a host of Bellbirds feeding in this mountain fairyland at treeline. The grey-beard forest ended abruptly as if the god of the mountains said, "Halt! Advance not!"

We were out beyond the trees into an alpine meadow where we could see forever. Ruth and I elected to admire the rocks and enjoy the alpine flowers while our companions went off to waste a pair of goats that were just spots on a distant mountain slope. The high country was a botanist's paradise. We chuckled gleefully and exclaimed as our eyes focussed on another and yet another new plant. Most spectacular, but looking out of place was a tall herb, the *Spaniard*, a distant relative of the pineapple, now in full bloom. The ground end of this beauty was a bunch, about two feet in diameter, of deceptively soft, thin, grey-green leaves. The points of these leaves were as sharp as steel needles and could puncture a finger at the slightest touch, as we soon found out. From the centre of the clump a stout stem shot up to a height of five feet. Flowers were massed along the stem with short bayonet blades protecting each blossom. These formidable candlesticks, towering over all the other ground-hugging herbage, covered the plateau as far as the eye could see. The scene was more like the high desert plateaux of Arizona or Mexico rather than a mountain top above the treeline in New Zealand.

Why did this unfriendly plant develop in these mountains where no grazing mammal trod the sod before European settlement? The answer lies with the bones of the Moas, giant flightless birds that roamed these islands until the Maoris arrived. There were many species ranging in volume from turkey-size to the gigantic eight-foot-tall *Dinornis maximus*. For millions of years these wonderful birds grazed and browsed their paths from sea level to alpine meadow. The first Maori settlers must have thought they had landed at a butcher shop with the door wide open. Can a hungry person keep hands off a mega turkey? Man's appetite for fresh meat was the birds' doom. Every day was Thanksgiving Day. Perhaps a few of these birds still survived in remote places as recently as two hundred years ago.

Ruth picking tobacco.

7

NEW ZEALAND FAREWELL

We were enjoying a high fat breakfast of *snorkers* and eggs in the sparsely-populated dining room on board the *Monowai*, riding the heaving Tasman Sea, out of Wellington, NZ, bound for Sydney, OZ. The passage between NZ and OZ is famous for rough water and *wog* stomachs. A few passengers who hate to miss a meal, were hanging over the rail hurling *chum* to the numerous sea fowl. Huge Wandering Albatrosses of the Southern Ocean, gliding on air waves humping up over the swells, followed the ship. Sometimes as many as twelve seemed to be attached to us by invisible lines. The smaller, graceful Black-browed Albatross was with us too, and there was a host of lesser stuff. Bat-like fluttering

petrels swept past on the wind, and endless lines of stiff-winged shearwaters cut the wave crests.

On the after-deck, a refuge from the wind and spray, watching shearwaters skimming over the bumps and hollows, we could feel the excitement of landing on a new shore tomorrow; excitement dampened by waves of nostalgia for the year of carefree wandering we left behind. We had biked and camped from the cannonading surf of Ninety Mile Beach to rugged Fiordland of the south. We reminisced about birds, hot springs, volcanic scenery, lonely shores and sombre forests. But most of all we remembered the friendly people of that pleasant pastoral land. We had made some good friends in New Zealand, many in the Motueka Valley we had so recently departed. There was K.J., the tobacco farm boss, who served us hot scones and generous tots of rum on those trying wet days that happened late in the season; the Peters, who lived across the creek, and Francis and Allan with whom we hiked the Tasman Mountains.

Our last adventure with Francis and Allan had been a Captain Cooker hunt the Sunday before we left the farm. We are not hunters but this invitation was a last chance for a trek into the back-country and, perhaps, to experience a wild pig encounter. Hog hunting was a popular weekend sport in New Zealand. Pigs were abundant and on the shite list of foresters, conservationists and farmers. They root up pastures, devour rare native plants and tree seedlings; they scarf eggs and young of ground-nesting birds and even have a taste for new-born lambs. *Sport hunting* for wild boar was done with well-trained dogs that *bail up* the victim, holding it until the hunter, armed with only a knife, arrives to dispatch it. Considering the impossible terrain, the dense vegetation and the known fighting ability of the boar, the animal has a sporting chance of surviving or at least inflicting a dose of serious injury on its attacker. I know of no other sport hunting where the hunted has the odds in its favour. Allan said he had finished off many a Captain Cooker in that traditional manner.

We were well into the Tasman foothills when dawn broke over the mountains. It was a glorious day, but perhaps not for the porkers we would meet later. We watched Allan's two dogs, directed only by low whistles and hand signals, quartering and covering the bracken-clad gullies. A pig had no place to hide but there seemed to be no pork in *them hills*.

Then all hell broke loose. From deep in the shoulder-high bracken, the solitude was shattered by the howling of two dogs and the grunting and squealing of pigs. Perhaps the dogs had a Captain Cooker bailed up. Allan was concerned about his dogs, as these wild boars are formidable beasts. With this in mind we attempted to crash our passage into the almost impenetrable ferns. Waving fern tops indicated not just one animal but perhaps a whole family. In bracken up to my chin I saw the waving fern-tops approaching directly towards me. Dog or pig? The commotion was only ten feet away. I could hear heavy breathing, not mine. Mine had stopped. Standing there with a .22 rifle, I felt like a blind man in a bull ring. Would the animal charge right through my legs venting its justifiable anger with a savage thrust with its four-inch tusks at my vulnerable anatomy? There was a moment of calm. Then the crack of Allan's .303 stirred my razorback friend into action. A terrified hog charged past me taking the lint off my corduroy pants with its bristles.

Allan shouted that he had a wounded pig beneath a hawthorn tree

Roast pork tonight.

only a few yards away. Blundering and thrashing through the vegetation, I was not prepared for a sudden eight-foot drop. In a most undignified manner I skidded to muddy stop, flat on my back, among two frenzied dogs, a wounded boar and a knife-wielding Allan.

We sat back and watched the professional way that Allan butchered the carcass. The hot sun was bringing out countless friendly bluebottles and an army of belligerent yellow jacket wasps arrived to carry off the blow-flies. Allen had proved his hunting ability; next his culinary skill. We protested. It will be tough. *You can't get your fork in the gravy.* And perhaps the meat will be loaded with every parasitic worm – round, flat and three cornered, known and unknown.

"Leave the cooking to me," Allan replied. "Tonight you will have a memorable farewell dinner and the worms, if any, will be well done."

Allan was right. A memorable dinner, or tea, as it is called in NZ, was on the table at seven. The gods on Mt. Olympus dined on nectar and ambrosia but as far as we were concerned that stuff couldn't hold a candle to *Captain Cooker à la Allan* – properly-prepared, bracken-fed wild New Zealand pork. The recipe: Take one medium-sized Tasman Mountain Captain Cooker, season to taste. And all the garnishes too – fried onions and mashed potatoes fresh from the farm soil, gravy and a tossed green salad. Dessert was banana rock melon. Finally, with mugs of scalding hot tea we stretched out around the roaring fireplace. We reminisced and recapitulated. It had been a wonderful but pensive farewell to New Zealand.

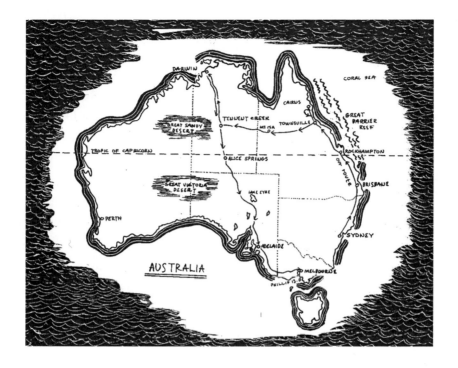

8

SUNRISE IN SUNNY NEW SOUTH

It was a dawn that will stick with me forever. Our ship was barely moving on a dead flat sea, the first calm day of the crossing. The sky was crystal clear with a faint tinge of red. When the sun burst up from the South Pacific the cirrus clouds now visible draped the sky with lines and mare's tails of red and gold. A reddish flat land framed by sharp cliffs adorned with spreading olive-drab trees lay ahead. Land, sea and sky seamed to blend together as we drew closer. Soon we sailed between the heads and entered one of the world's finest natural harbours. We passed under the famous bridge so dear to the hearts of Australians, particularly Sydneysiders. We had arrived. It was warm and dry; a biker's delight. Hello, Australia!

Peter and Margaret, who had been in Australia for more than a month, met us on the pier and directed us to inexpensive accommodation on the Manly shore. As housing in both Australia and New Zealand was scarce and expensive, we were happy to have a roof over our heads so quickly. We had a small bedroom with shared kitchen and toilet facilities. Now we had time to see the city and plan our travels. We left our motorcycle and a tea chest full of camping gear in the customs shed and boarded one of the delightful harbour ferries to Manly, a pleasant suburb where tall Norfolk Island pines framed the beach.

Our landlady, known to us transients as *Mrs. Lavish McTavish*, was the very epitome of frugality. Or was she a dedicated environmentalist? She rented small bedrooms at one pound a night to both temporary and permanent guests. When we arrived she was gleefully rubbing her hands together thinking about the influx of visitors for the Easter holidays and the Royal Easter Show. Her establishment was run on *tight lines*, to quote a fisherman's expression. Guests shared the kitchen under the watchful eyes of the landlady, ever alert to turn off the gas as soon as the kettle began to boil or the frying pan started to crackle, even though we paid an extra seven bob a week for this privilege. Light bulbs were the lowest wattage obtainable (about three candle power) and spaced at maximum distance. It was just possible to read newspaper headlines if you were blessed with 20/20 vision. The newspapers, mostly unread, were gathered from the guests' bedrooms for use as toilet paper. Newspaper, cut into six-inch squares, impaled on a long cord hung from the ceiling at the sitting person's eye level, was a feature of the bathrooms and an example of frugal recycling, especially since the newspapers represented the guests' cash.

A favourite dodge of our landlady's was to ask for the teapot after we had finished dinner. There might be a cupful left or more likely just some well-stewed leaves but, no matter, add boiling water, let it sit and there was her cup of tea! Once we informed our landlady that we had friends coming in and we would be making tea about 11:00 p.m. We wanted her to realize that we were honest folk with no intentions of subletting for the night or raiding the larder. Her reply: "What a shame, you have just emptied your teapot."

The milk-bottle episode really took the prize. Mrs Lavish insisted that she set out our bottles on the step each night. We were touched by her thoughtfulness that went beyond the call of duty and paid her the eleven pence hap'ny per bottle she asked. Later we learned that milk was eleven pence. She charged us a half penny for her labour.

Our abode did have some very fine features. It was in a quiet neighbourhood, a point emphasised daily by Mrs. Lavish. From the dining room we had great views of the sunset over Sydney Harbour. Manly's shopping centre was only a short walk away. There were beaches on either side of the main street – surf on one side, sheltered bathing on the other. Manly's aquarium nearby, displaying some of Australia's large and carnivorous aquatic denizens, was a warning to the timid visitor to stay well above the tide line.

Sydney was a city with personality and congestion. Narrow streets and tall buildings gave us a feeling of being at the bottom of a canyon. At several intersections, the traffic, consisting mostly of Holdens, the Aussie General Motors product, was directed by mounted policemen. On our short stay in the big city we were tourists visiting and gazing at Sydney's famous sights: the bridge, the zoo, the Domain and King's Cross. One of the bulging-eye and mouth-watering sights was the mountains of delicious fruit from temperate and tropical zones piled high on barrows at every street corner. For variety and flavour Australian fruit takes first place every time.

We stayed in Sydney for a fortnight. I took a three-day job at the Elinora Golf and Country Club, relieving the janitor away on holiday, and came away richer by twelve pounds and a bath towel.

9

SIGHTS AND SOUNDS
OF THE AUSTRALIAN BUSH

Finally, one morning in late April, under a clear blue sky, we said goodbye to our parsimonious landlady, saddled up and hit the road again. We planned a slow ride north along the New South Wales shore. We were here to see what there was to see, not to get there. The scenery was pleasant but not spectacular. There was an overall lack of colour in the endless eucalyptus trees but there were subtle changes and moods that are not readily apparent to the hurried traveller. This was not the sombre majesty of the New Zealand forests where man seems out of place, nor was it the soft friendly atmosphere of the European woods where seasonal changes are the rule. This was a different world.

The Australian bush is an open, airy domain; a world of brittle light where variety and beauty is not in colourful foliage but in the trunks of the trees. Gum trees, so alike from a distance, break up into numerous distinctive boles when viewed at close quarters. These trees are evergreen, shedding long slender leaves only when new leaves are already in place. Many shed their bark in long peeling strips of red and gold festoons, contrasting with the greens and yellows of the new bark beneath. Most trees of the gum family, comprising over four hundred species, are tall and spreading. The wattles of the lower forest layer barely reach their shoulders. Banksias with upstanding flowers like bottle brushes dominate the bottom story. Down at ground level there are patches of red earth, grass, ant cities and sandy paths.

In the wetter valleys the scene is decidedly tropical. Here, the open gum tree woodland was replaced by palms and lianas in choking profusion. Sometimes we had vistas of the blue South Pacific rolling in on white sandy beaches below red sandstone cliffs. Settlements were scarce along the coast. In the valleys, cows grazed; northward, sugar cane in the lowlands and banana plantations hugged the hillsides.

The birds were fabulous! Braking to a sudden stop, propping the bike against a tree, we dashed into the forest or the grassy margins of swamps after parrots or spoonbills. The open woodlands were favoured by aggressive birds in black and white dress. Here was the friendly, noisy Magpie-lark which we found from Sydney's parks to the shores of the Timor Sea. Lots of the Australian Magpies, white-backed in the south, black-backed in the north, carolling in the treetops. Family groups of comical Choughs hopped about on the ground. When alarmed they flew up to perch, spreading and elevating their tails in an eye-catching manner. Two species of butcherbird, one grey, the other pied, both excellent songbirds, were eye and ear catchers. Crow-sized Black Currawongs flitting through the open glades called out their names – *currawong – currawong*. Members of the honey-eater tribe – leather-headed Noisy Friar Birds and curved-beaked Eastern Spine-bills foraged in the banksias and wattle. The honey eaters are almost as diversified as the gum trees on which they depend for sustenance. In the undergrowth the male Eastern Whipbird uttered his extraordinary whip cracks followed by his mate's more subdued *chew – chew*. And there was plenty of other stuff – kingfishers, cuckoo-shrikes, whistlers and babblers.

In the bird kingdom one species is the jester. This fellow is the Kookaburra, the world's largest kingfisher, at home in the dry uplands, sombre in plumage but a champion in laughter. The rollicking laughter of the *Laughing Jackass* or *Settler's Alarm Clock* can be heard at any time of day but it is most likely and appreciated just as the first faint glimmer of dawn hits the tree tops: a signal for all the world's diurnal wild creatures to sing, yawn, scratch, yodel, defecate and find breakfast. The kook's vocalizing, which must be heard to be believed, is often voiced by a pair or a family group. Then it is really marvellous. Sitting on a gum tree branch, heads thrown back, bodies vibrating, they seem to be sharing a huge joke known only to themselves: first just a chuckle, then uncontrolled riotous laughter. Kookaburras are at home in suburban gardens as well as the woodlands. New immigrants from southern Europe, where birds are appreciated only in the frying pan, have been accused of making a snack of the *ha-ha pigeon*. In the tropical north, the Blue-winged Kookaburra has brighter plumage but a second-rate laughter. In movies and TV the kookaburra's mirth is a familiar sound heard in tropical adventure shows taking place in Africa and South America.

Parrots! Wow! The Casuarinas were loaded with Rainbow Lorikeets; slow-flapping flocks of Sulphur-crested Cockatoos were overhead. Galahs were passing over, their pink breasts illuminated by the dawn's early light.

Every marsh and estuary was stuffed with birds. Ducks of different feathers, Black Swans and Maned Geese congregated in the open water while curved-billed ibises, stately white egrets, solemn herons and quaint spoonbills of two species – Yellow-billed and Royal stalked the margins. Roosting flocks festooned the mangroves. With the aid of six-inch toes, Jacanas, also known as Lilly-Trotters or Christ Birds walked nonchalantly on the lotus pads. In flight, with out-sized feet trailing, they looked comical indeed. Cormorants, drying out-stretched wings, perched on tall snags. Amongst them sat Australian Darters or Snake Birds with snake-like necks and long tails also drying out after an early morning's fishing expedition. Scavenging Square-tailed Kites and beautiful Brahminy Kites circled overhead. Sometimes the sky was ornamented by a huge White-breasted Sea Eagle tracing lazy circles.

"Look at those pompous guys," exclaimed Ruth, pointing to a row of plump birds in a green pasture. "They look like a regiment of nineteenth century soldiers on parade in full dress."

They were Spur-winged Plovers, all facing in the same direction and formed up in line abreast as if under the stern eye of a sergeant major! Black caps, epaulets, white chests and showy yellow wattles indicated a military species. They were armed too. On the leading edge of each wing they carried a business-like bayonet, called a spur, with which they could knock the stuffing out of any bird or beast silly enough to try to molest their eggs or young.

The daily wonders of the Australian bush and the thrill of seeing new birds continued as we slowly moved north, brewing up and making camp beside billabongs, until one evening we rode into Queensland's boom town, Surfer's Paradise, known as the Miami of the Southern Hemisphere. Here we had the only flat tire of the trip, fortunately right beside a small garage.

To sample the surf and have a rest from bush and birds we went in search of a spreading gum tree under which we would pitch our tent. We found the right spot at the public campground in the pleasant town of Southport. We had barely settled in when our next-door neighbours, an elderly brother and sister couple, showed up, to educate us about everything: the prevailing winds, Labour's chances in the next election, where to buy inexpensive vegetables, the risk of becoming a shark's dinner at Surfer's and so on without a break. They had roamed Australia from Wollongong to Warrnambool and from Koolpinyah to Koo-Wee-Rup in an old bus fixed up to become a house on wheels. They followed

Waltzing Matilda

Once a jolly swagman camped by a
billabong
Under the shade of a coolibah tree,
And he sang as he watched and
waited till his billy boiled,
You'll come a-waltzing, Matilda, with
me.

Chorus:

"Waltzing Matilda, waltzing Matilda.
You'll come a-waltzing, Matilda with
me."
And he sang as he watched and
waited till his billy boiled,
"You'll come' a-waltzing, Matilda,
with me."

Down came a jumbuck to drink at that
billabong,
Up jumped the swagman and
grabbed him with glee,
And he sang as he shoved that jumbuck in his tucker bag,
"You'll come a-waltzing, Matilda,
with me."

Down came the squatter, mounted on
his thoroughbred,
Down came the troopers, one, two,
three,
"Where's the jolly jumbuck you've got
in your tucker bag?
You'll come a-waltzing, Matiida,
with me."

Up jumped the swagman and sprang
into the billabong,
"You'll never catch me alive,"
said he,
And his ghost may be heard as you
pass by that billabong,
"You'll come a-waltzing, Matilda,
with me."

the sun or the shade depending on the seasons and the chances of casual work. True Gypsies.

Seeing our blackened billy can and frying pan sitting on a dry stick fire, our new friends insisted we use their stove, fry our steaks and sample their Aussie Red. We were pleased and appreciated their hospitality. The next three days were exact replica of the first. The monologue continued non-stop, punctuated at intervals with our: "Well, that's very interesting; we are off to the beach now."

But it was almost impossible to get away from the torrent of Australiana. Those two were certainly interesting and knowledgeable people, but they were beyond a doubt Australia's champion *ear bashers* and that title does not come easy Down Under.

One day, seeking a change, we rode up on the high ground toward Lamington. Below, the landscape was dry and brown, around us, green grass and big trees. Here we saw numerous Monarch Butterflies among the *swan trees*, a giant species of milk-weed on which their larva fed. The seed capsules of this plant look like miniature swans complete with curved neck, hence the name. The Monarch, an American butterfly, is now common in parts of both Australia and New Zealand.

After a cool drink, under gum trees animated by Noisy Friar Birds in the Nerang beer garden, we rode into a trailer camp near Brisbane. We were not welcome. The caretaker let us know in a patronizing manner that, "This establishment does not cater to swaggies [Australian tramps or bums]." After a lecture on social values she condescended to let us stay, but first she must measure our tent. It seemed that a person's social standing was directly proportional to the size of his or her tent. By now we were feeling like a pair of peddlers sneaking up the front steps of Buckingham Palace. We'd had enough. I kicked the starter and we were off in a shower of small stones, leaving Mrs Upsnout unfurling her tape measure. I refrained from pointing a finger skyward.

In Brisbane, where a young reporter from the *Courier Mail* found us, we were directed to a rustic campground at Sandgate. It was pleasant but wind-swept, but there was water on tap and plenty of dry wood for the picking. Campers were few, birdlife on the vast tidal flats was excellent and the site was free! Paradise couldn't be better.

Riding north from Brisbane we passed through thick fruit planta-tions where roadside stand were piled high with bananas, pineapples, oranges and tomatoes. New to us were custard apples and a fruit called *Monsterio deliscioso*. We pigged out daily. Life was good but the roads got worse.

Bitumen was scarce. Sometimes we were confused by a series of trails with not a sign post to indicate the way. We wanted to hug the coast, and we succeeded only after multiple wrong turns. In those long ago days people got lost in northern Queensland. White stakes with num-bers in feet at either end of concrete dips marked watercourses. We had to imagine that there might be five feet and up of running water over these fords during *the Wet*. Now the country-side was dry as a popcorn fart.

Water fit for drinking was a bit of a problem as we carried only an ex-army water bottle. Since creeks, some brackish, some dry and others just a succession of pools were common along the coast, we took a risk with our water supply. Anytime in the afternoon we kept a sharp eye peeled for a pleasant camping spot beside a billabong. A good camp was impor-tant; time on the road was not. Beneath rustling paperbark trees beside a muddy water hole, we pitched our little tent and brewed up a full billy of industrial strength tea. We believed that the boil-up would at least weaken the microbes, parasites and other nasties before the nectar got to our dehydrated guts. The night descended abruptly about six o'clock. While it was light we watched gaudy parrots, funereal Black Cockatoos and turkey-size Australian Bustards coming in for their nightly drink.

We always selected a campsite clear of ant cities. Australia has more than its share of ants, some big and aggressive. A particularly war-like bunch lives in a cluster of short gravel mounds with connecting trails as devoid of vegetation as a cow path. The combined pit-a-pat of a million ant feet moving in a solid stream at the speed of a walking person creates an audible sound.

Night under thin canvas in a new country is exciting and sometimes scary. What bird or beast is responsible for those eerie grunts, rumbles and hoots? Lying close to the earth magnifies the thumping of wallabies hopping about on their crepuscular foraging. Owls called nightly for *more pork*. A skein of migrating Magpie Geese gabbled overhead. Brolgas trumpeted in the distance. On the outback plains of Queensland we heard the sad wailing, *wee-loo, wee-loo* of Stone Curlews; melancholy spirit wailing of aboriginal hunters of the long ago. Sometimes the night creaking was only a couple of old trees rubbing their butts together.

One night we were awakened to a sinister *Oom, Oom,* from the tree-tops above our tent. What was it? Slowly opening the tent flap I shone our torch into the thin foliage. Nothing but the trade wind rustling leathery gum tree leaves. We dug out our copy of Cayley's *What Bird is That?* After some searching we found it: Our midnight caller was a Tawny Frogmouth, a bird that is often misidentified as just another bump on a log, as it fits its environment so well. Another time we heard a mysterious thump, a bump and a rasp right at our front door. I untied one tape, shone the torch, and peering out was eyeball-to-eyeball with a weird rat-faced wallaby.

There are, nevertheless, those night sounds that defy explanations: perhaps, the baying of beasts unknown to science or perhaps, the guttural growls of goblins? It was 2:00 a.m. on the wet tropical coast south of Cairns. We were snug in our tent in a perfect campsite on the bank of Sunday Creek opposite Hinchinbrook Island. We were awakened by a sudden sharp downpour and a rush of wind through the trees. Then the night silence returned except for an unusual gulping noise like a large carnivore belching after swallowing a sheep. We listened, somewhat concerned as the loud gulps and burps coming from the direction of the creek continued. The creature sounding-off seemed to be moving about too. Armed with flashlight and a two-foot-long machete we crawled out to find the monster before it found us. It must be identified. At the river-bank we heard another belch apparently coming from under water. We were surprised to see the creek, only a trickle the evening

North into the tropics.

before, now a wide river flowing inland. And there, in a swirling pool, was a huge black body with four long horns. We were face to face with a Bunyip, Australia's version of the Loch Ness Monster. The Bunyip, magnified in the flashlight's circle in the surrounding blackness, was coming directly at us, burping as it closed in. Almost at our feet the monster metamorphosed into a dead cow, belly up, bloated like a barrage balloon. The four horns were its stiff legs pointing skyward. The burps and gulps remained a mystery until morning when the tidal creek was back to a mere trickle again. In the many caves and hollows in the banks, air was trapped by the inrushing tide. The escaping gas produced the scary belches we heard during the night. Perhaps these noises were magnified by the calm night and our imaginations. This episode illustrates how easy it is to create those unnatural beasts that are always popping up their out-of-focus bodies from lakes and swamps. Nessie fessie, Ogopogo smogo! No wonder our tea tasted salty last night.

Just south of Rockhampton we crossed the tropic of Capricorn. We were now officially in the Torrid Zone. We were on the Bruce Highway: next facilities, one hundred and twenty miles. Topping a rare rise we saw the vast plain of Capricorn stretching from here to infinity. In the hazy northern horizon purple hills met the sky. It was a dry sun-burnt land; a land of high brown grass and low gnarled trees of the stringy bark and iron bark varieties. New to us and unique to Australia was the grass tree with the scientific name *Xanthorrhoea* that conjures up bad visions of an unwelcome social disease. The common name for the grass tree at that time was *black-boy* because at a distance it looks like an Aboriginal person holding a tall spear. Another *new* and strange hunk of vegetation was the pot-bellied bottle tree, *Adansonia*.

Here, too, were a few twenty-foot-tall individuals of the prickly pear cactus, an American import that almost conquered Queensland before another assisted immigrant, *Cactoblastis*, a cactus-eating bug, devoured the unwanted plant by the square mile – a famous example of biological cavalry to the rescue. Miles of blackened earth testified to the extent of recent bush fires.

There was a sudden change to lush tropical vegetation and humid air when the road dropped down to the pleasant town of McKay. Bright green forests covered the hill-sides; tall thin palms outlined watercourses, farmsteads with papaws [papayas] and bananas beckoned. It was time for a rest and another fruit orgy.

We put up at a pleasant campsite bounded by the sea on one side; mangroves and lagoons on the others. Birds? Fantastic! But before we tackled the birds we decided to have showers and a much needed change of laundry. In the trees we saw Spangled Drongos, Fig Birds and Varied Trillers; in the lagoons there were white egrets, huge Australian Pelicans and skinny legged Pied Stilts. The most unusual new bird was the tall, unreal Black-necked Stork, sometimes wrongly called *Jabiru*.

When the tide went out, the sea retreated beyond the horizon, leaving behind an enormous expanse of sand and mud, exposing a cornucopia of goodies for animals higher up on the food ladder. While observing curlews and Golden plovers fattening up for the long flight to the Siberian Arctic, we were impressed by the sight of armies of miniature blue football helmets marching and counter marching across the muddy sand. These armies were hordes of soldier crabs, one of the amazing denizens of the tropic shore. Acres of pigeon-egg-sized crustaceans. Columns a hundred yards long and ten feet across moved methodically over the strand, rolling the sand into millions of tiny balls in the process of sucking up the microscopic life living therein. When danger threatened, such as was the case when we incautiously approached, the little soldiers vanished in a second by the simple process of *digging a hole and pulling the hole in over themselves*. Digging out a plug of sand they rolled into the hole and pulled the plug over, a quick and complete vanishing act. Standing quiet for a few minutes we saw the beach come to life again as thousands of little blue crabs appeared simultaneously. Several times we saw tragedy strike. One of their enemies is a large mud crab. This cunning fellow holes up in a soggy place without leaving a trace. When a soldier treads on the big guy's lair the mud crab, sensing the proximity of dinner, shoots out two armoured claws, seizes the little guy and devours him on the spot to the accompaniment of loud crackling noises.

In the mangrove coast of north Queensland we saw colourful fiddler crabs that live in burrows in the sticky mud. These crabs excavate their dens by rolling up balls of mud the size of hen's eggs. The balls are deposed in rings around the burrow, in time, making a mound of considerable size. In some places where the tidal extremes are thirty feet or more, large areas of mangrove are inundated only twice a month. During the ten days between spring tides the fiddler lives in its cool den, the entrance to which is plugged with a ball of mud. When high tide deposits another layer of organic mud the crab emerges to feed.

We spent some fascinating hours watching fiddler crabs having lunch. There were hundreds within a few yards, each with its own burrow into which it retreated at any sign of danger. The fiddler-on-the mud is an individualist, feeding only within a short radius of its own lair; not moving as a carpet like the soldier crab. First you see an enormous brilliant claw blocking the crab's hole. Then a relatively small animal appears with a tiny delicate second claw. Using its tiny claw it begins stuffing its mouth with microscopic mud-loving delicacies. The steady, rhythmical motion behind the oversize claw gives this animal its name. It is a perfect miniature likeness of a fiddler.

10

TROPICAL DAZE IN QUEENSLAND NORTH

Between McKay and Cairns (pronounced *Cains*) there were many landscape changes. Along the narrow coastal plain, green fields of sugar cane stretched for miles while the mountain slopes were thick with matted green forests with the ridiculous name of *big scrub*. At Townsville the dry inland savannah came down to the coast. The roads, which aged our motorcycle and us considerably, were often only a series of potholes connected by mounds of gravel. The innumerable narrow gauge railway crossings were another hazard. These railroads, carrying haystack loads of sugar cane to the crushing mills, crossed the highway with disconcerting frequency and suddenness, usually on a blind corner or at the bottom of a hill. Fortunately for us the cane harvest had only started. Otherwise, perhaps, our journey would have ended short of *Cains*.

Cairns for us was a landmark destination. We rode down to the beach expecting to see the Great Barrier Reef at our feet. The tide was out exposing a vast grey expanse of mud with only a solitary white egret and a scattering of mangrove sprouts breaking the monotony. There was some talk about reclamation of this *unused land* for commercial purposes. In season these mud flats are important refuelling stations for thousands of Eurasian shore birds *en route* to and from Australia and Siberia. (I emphasised this to the local newspaper reporter.)

To see the reef we had to take a short boat excursion to Green Island. At 9:00 am we were on board crammed in with at least two hundred others, mostly elderly tourists from the south. The seniors covered every inch of deck space, soaking up the rays while the children romped below. Rounding the mangrove-covered headland we encountered a severe weather change. A brisk south-east trade wind and strong tidal currents were churning up a remarkably choppy sea. Without warning the bow seemed to go straight down allowing a sizable wall of water to crash over the upper deck. Women screamed, men cursed; everyone was instantly waterlogged. Another wave lashed over, catching everyone on their feet hurrying to reach shelter, a difficult and dangerous manoeuvre on a small boat pitching and rolling in a heaving sea. After much confusion, lots of screaming and even more cursing the human cargo was below deck standing shoulder to shoulder and belly to back. The hatches were closed to keep the boat from filling up and sinking. The air became foul; the rolling, pitching and yawling got worse. A greenish wash was spreading over many faces, even those who had spent a lifetime at sea. Ruth staggered down below to join the lineup at the *Ladies*. Soon some unhappy souls, unable to move, were up-chucking where they stood. Standing in the crowded aisle and hanging on to an overhead deck beam, I viewed the agonies of my fellow travellers with that look of amused tolerance that *those who aren't* regard *those who are*. But the motion, the thick air and the example of others finally took effect.

I was determined to bear up, trying to preserve the allusion that I was enjoying the voyage, but I was forced to surrender. Fortunately, I made it to the heads in time and took my turn over the wash basins with the others.

The boat emptied quickly once we were back on good hard ground where sea sickness, unlike most other maladies, vanished. The captain said, "Welcome to Green Island" and added "I have never seen anything like that before." Nowadays, one can blame tricky weather and almost anything else on El Niño (known at that time only to people on the coast of Peru) or Global Warming (not yet invented.)

Palm-ringed Green Island was a Queensland government tourist resort for day trippers eager to see the Great Barrier Reef's wonders. The major attraction, the underwater observatory, built by Vince Vlasoff and Lloyd Grigg, was opened for marine gawkers in June 1954. The observatory, constructed of three-inch steel plate, reinforced with ten-inch steel girders with a total weight of one hundred tons, is twenty-five feet long, eight feet wide and seven feet high. Large windows, made of one-and-one eighth-inch plate glass, allow for superb views of the reef's denizens. The observatory, perhaps, the world's best at that time, proved to be a real winner and probably still is. At sixteen feet below the sea we were captivated by a plethora of marine creatures engaged in the timeless game of eat and be eaten. We were looking out at the fishes; the fishes were looking in at us.

Lunch at the tourist hotel was a tepid, greasy mutton stew, served by a waitress with a *take it or leave it* attitude. There was no attempt to exploit the tropic isle atmosphere by employing grass-skirted belles serving exotic dishes as is the custom in Hawaii. We expected to get the finger on the way out as our tip was microscopic. In the afternoon we fossicked over the beaches with the other tourists while bent-winged frigate birds hung in the sky overhead and white herons stabbed at fishes in the shallows.

Cairns was good for a long stop to enjoy the tropical scene. We pitched our Egyptian cotton shelter at the town campground and settled in even though the primitive outhouse holes were inadequate for the *on-slot* of hordes of tourists and transients who visit this tourist-Mecca of North Queensland. The method of collecting camping fees was unique and seemed hardly fair. Once a week a city official appeared demanding a week's pay regardless of the amount of ground you covered or the number of days spent on it. The unlucky sod on the spot paid for the dodger who bolted between rounds.

Other than our mild gripes over toilets and fees, Cairns was a real paradise for travelling naturalists. We even enjoyed the daily tropical pelt down although it usually occurred just as we were getting *stuck into* our dinner of Aussie steak, fresh pineapple and hot tea. These heavy showers approaching from the east, produced, with the setting sun, rainbows of exceptional perfection and brilliance. The bows moved closer with the rain until the curtain of rain and the bow, perhaps only a hundred yards away, connected with our ground. Once, behind the rain, a full moon rose treating us to a lunar rainbow in the west – a beautiful but eerie phenomenon. This happened less than an hour after we watched a spectacular solar bow approaching from the east. When the storm rolled away, Orion dipped behind the western mountains, Scorpio rose in the east and the Southern Cross swung up to the zenith. Sprawled across the northern sky was the Great Bear or Charles's Wain. We were excited to see this constellation again after an absence of thirteen months.

At Cairns we got bitten by the collecting bug, a disease common to mankind but ridiculous in our case as we were drifters with no fixed abode. All those pretty seashells and exquisite butterflies! We could arrange shells in front of our tent, making it homier, even artsy. Butterflies we wanted to see at close range and perhaps identify. Shells we could pick up on the beach, butterflies had to be netted. We rode out to Yorkey's Knob one morning with visions of hundreds of colourful shells littering the tide line. We found a mixture of broken and sand-blasted specimens except for a fine large bailer which was hurrying along a muddy patch at a speed unusual for a mollusc. We grabbed it and found it was the mobile home of a feisty hermit crab. It didn't seem sporting to oust the hermit with his vulnerable backside, to face the dangerous beach. We left it in peace and returned home with a few not too battered treasures. The vast arrays of mollusc shells you see in tropical beach shops are obtained from living animals that are becoming scarce due to over collecting.

Now for the butterflies. The north Queensland rain forest is butterfly heaven – blues, whites, swallowtails, bird-wings. We wanted closer views of the gorgeous bird-wings and other big fellows that flitted high in the treetops. Armed with a crude net made from cheese cloth taped onto a bailing wire hoop nailed to a long mangrove pole, we set out for the forested slopes where butterflies were abundant. I flailed the air for nearly an hour before I brought down a beautiful bird-wing. It would be a fine trophy pinned up outside our tent. Perish the thought! In hand was a magnificent product of millions of years of evolution or a masterpiece created by intelligent design in seven days yet, only four thousand years ago. Whatever. It was a beautiful living thing. We watched it flap up to the canopy to carry on with its happy(?) life. It made us realise how fortunate we were to be alive to share and appreciate this world of stately trees and butterfly jewels. Our short collecting mode was over.

Cairns cast its spell. Why leave? Well, even our decidedly frugal lifestyle required an injection of money. Perhaps there were jobs right here in the sugar fields. Work for awhile, save some money, enjoy the north, and move on later.

Early one morning I arrived at the Commonwealth Employment Office with another twelve hundred would-be sugar workers.

Man behind the counter, "What experience have you had?"

Me: "None."

Gruff and to the point, "Well, you haven't a hope in Hell of getting work here. This year we have the biggest influx of southern workers since the war, and next week we have a shit-load [or did he say shipload?] of Sicilian cane cutters arriving. Later, when the season gets underway, there might be an opening for a sugar lumper. Plenty of overtime too," he added.

I'm thinking: sugar lumper? I'll go for that. Mindlessly moulding little lumps of sugar or, perhaps, counting the cubes as they drop off the conveyer belt. Lots of time for meditation, perhaps even checking the bird field guides.

"What's a sugar lumper?" I asked.

"Carrying and stacking one hundred pound sacks of sugar at the loading dock."

Another wilting look from The Man. "What the bloody hell did you think it was, mate?"

"Next," he said, eyeing the muscle-bound sod next in line.

Bye, bye! I'll pass on that one. Later when I saw an army of Sicilians clear-cutting a sugar field I realized that I wasn't built for cane bashing. These guys were short (bending over was no problem) and thick, with arm muscles like an anaconda that had just swallowed a sheep

And so we went back to communing with nature for another week.

That interview got me interested in sugar. I wanted find out more about this sweet and sticky stuff. Were there any peripheral jobs that offered a good reward in pounds, shillings and pence? I obtained a lot of conflicting information and even more wishful thinking, especially in the realm of employment. Cane cutting, I was told, was where the big money lay but this year there was no chance of breaking into the *racket*. At this I was thankful for cane cutting must be the dirtiest of the world's back-breaking jobs. The cane is fired before harvesting in order to get rid of surplus leaves, leaving a single stock for the knife-wielding cutter who whacks it off close to the ground. By day's end, a cane cutter, sweating in the humid heat and soot, is as black as a Bantu and totally knackered. Fire helps to rid the fields of snakes, insects and rats that have infiltrated the sweet jungle. Blazing cane attracts large birds and birdwatchers. At a distance one sees a column of black smoke with floating lumps. The lumps are birds. In the thick smoke and just above the flames, Black Kites wheel and pounce on barbecued insects and snakes while Straw-necked Ibises stalk the edges spearing any singed creature scrambling to safety. A feeding frenzy: an elemental play of fire, gourmet dining and death.

There is a long slim tree snake in this pandanus tree.

We retreated south to Townsville via the Atherton Tablelands. The ocean end of the trans-Queensland highway from Townsville to the Northern Territory and Darwin, was the only route west. The road over the Tablelands climbed through dense, metallic, broad-leaved evergreen rain forest. Absolutely magnificent! Below, a vast panorama of cane on the flats stopping only at the mangrove-framed ocean shores. In the afternoon we broke out of the forest onto a plateau of grass and cows. Here the old rain forest had been converted into grass, the raw material of milk and meat. Only isolated copse and white-trunked dead trees remained. The dead had stout branches reaching skyward – ghostly in the twilight –good perches for birds.

A grove of relict rain forest beckoned us to walk its barely visible paths. Here were giant fig trees, their smooth buttressed trunks like columns holding up a closed roof of leaves. We learned from our books that several deadly tree species lurk in Queensland's rain forests. The fruit of the finger cherry, *Rhodomystus macrocarpa*, can cause blindness if eaten.

It may be a fungus on the fruit rather than the fruit itself that is to blame, as some people have shown no ill effects after a snack. The fruit and leaves of the corkwood, *Duboisia myoporoides*, may cause blindness and death. This plant, like derris, *Derris trifoliata*, is used to stun fish. But the meanest of all the nasty trees, *Laportea sp.* must have been designed by nature in one of her malevolent moods. *Laportea*, mother of all stinging nettles, has heart-shaped leaves from five inches to a foot in length covered with tiny, prickly hairs which can cause extreme pain on contact with naked skin. There are tales, probably true, of both man and horse driven mad after a swipe from this tree. There is even a story of one or more soldiers on a military exercise during WW II using *Laportea* leaves for bum fodder. That is too awful to contemplate.

There is another sinister member of the arborescent world, the Tar Tree or Tree of Death. One does not have to eat the fruit or leaves of this plant to come to a sad end. Merely sleeping or resting beneath its shade may invite blistered skin and blindness, for filtering down from the canopy is a powerful irritant dust.

Why are some plants so dangerous? Plants have had to develop many ways to protect themselves from the hairy, feathery and scaly vegetarian hordes that would eat them to extinction. Nevertheless, it seems that Queensland's trees have developed protection to the extreme, considering the absence of multitudes of leaf eaters, except for a few cassowaries and possums. Perhaps, the answer can be found in the past when for millions of years plants were evolving with a much greater and varied mega fauna. The animal enemies were doomed to extinction by man's insatiable appetite for fresh meat beginning only thirty thousand years ago when the first colonists walked in to Australia during the last ice age. The vegetation is still armed and dangerous but their enemies are long gone.

A cold wind blowing up from the South Pole was sweeping over the Tablelands. Although we were only seventeen degrees below the equator, we were shivering. When the sun dropped to the horizon the chill intensified. Beside a little creek in a clearing close to a farmstead we made camp. The tent was up, a fine fire blazing and a billy for tea on the boil. Life was good. While choking down the first mug of tea the lady of the house drove up.

"Come in to the house," she said. "You will freeze out here."

We declined the kind offer, saying we preferred sleeping out and we were looking forward to an exceptional starry night and the sounds of the bush.

She was right. We froze. Sunset brought heavy dew, and soon the frost gripped the earth. Our light cotton tent froze stiff. We were right about the stars though. The heavens that night, in the crystal-clear atmosphere of the plateau, were fabulous. Corvus was directly overhead; below, Crux Australis and the magnificent southern Milky Way with its black holes and misty lights. Far to the south the Magellanic Clouds shimmered while in the northeast Corona Borealis and Arcturus blazed. On the northern horizon Ursa Major enveloped half the sky. But the wonder of all was our first view of the Zodiacal Light that rose from its broad base on the western horizon to a peak at the zenith. Numb with cold, we crept into our sleeping bags fully dressed to find more stars. Our five-watt electric light created a whole heaven of frost stars sparkling inside our tent.

In the morning, aching and almost paralysed, we crept out to a fairy tale world. In the rising sun the tropical rain forest stood silent and ghostly, shrouded in thick hoar frost and rime and adorned with a million ice diamonds. The tall grass stems were bowed with frost crystals; the turf was white and crisp. A pair of snow white hawks circled overhead. Had we been transported to a land near the pole or was this a dream? Were we really only a thousand miles south of the equator? A flock of big, noisy green King Parrots arrived to feed on the berry bushes by the creek. The rime was melting. We were still in tropical Australia. It was time to get a fire started and brew up the billy.

We rode leisurely over the Tablelands enjoying the warm sun and the interaction with the wildlife that can only be appreciated at a slow pace. The mound building Australian Brush-turkey was a frequent flyer across our path. Victoria's Rifle Birds watched us from tall roadside trees. Once I had to crack on both brakes to avoid a dangerous collision with a big black Cassowary. The prize of the day was a Platypus, that crazy, mixed-up creature of the animal world. Well, that's what we think. The duck-bill, found only in Australia, from Victoria to Cairns, is about twenty inches long; it has a duck beak, a mammal's fur, lays eggs and suckles its young.

In late afternoon we could feel the cold air returning as only bikers can experience it. It was unanimous: we wouldn't spend another night here. Innisfail, on the coast; sugar cane, mangroves and humid heat would be our next campsite before sunset.

From Innisfail it was a short ride to Townsville and Rowe's Bay Tent and Trailer Park where we would spend the next five weeks. We were in need of a long stop in order to tool up for the journey across Queensland to Darwin. Motorcycle and gear were in need of repairs and fixings. Saddlebag frames, fabricated in New Zealand from dump-salvaged strap iron and plywood, were coming adrift in several places. A boulder had crumpled the exhaust muffler. Worst of all; a clanging in the motor seemed to be symptomatic of sickness in the big end bearing.

Deciding to go for a complete motor overhaul, I proceeded straight away to strip the engine. After two days of frustrating toil without proper tools and harassed by clouds of dust, I realized that I would have to seek help at the local bike shop. Foul language wasn't helping either. After listening to my hard luck tale, the shop foreman, a profoundly sympathetic man, offered me use of any special tools and gave me some very useful advice while I worked on the bike in the alley behind the shop. One of the essential tools for working on an engine is the vise. I was most grateful to the foreman for having access to this necessity. I was relieved to find the big end in good shape after all, but the bearing on the timing side was buggered. This was soon replaced; valves were ground, new rings fitted and the old Ariel was good for another five thousand miles of rough tracks and adventure. The crumpled exhaust was hammered out, and a Shell Oil can was pushed over the holes. It fitted beautifully. All other parts were purchased in the shop.

Next item on our list was temporary employment. Jobs for females were scarce except for: *Governess wanted, seven pounds a week and keep, at a distant cattle station*, and: *Experienced bar maid, live in, at Muttaburra*. Male employment was somewhat better. I landed a twelve pound a week *secure* job with the Gas and Coke Co, narrowly escaping an eleven pounds ten shillings sentence as a fettler. I thought a fettler was an Australian gandy-dancer or perhaps, horse's hoof doctor.

My new job didn't require much thinking, but it was fine for meditating and the pay was good. I spent the first few days behind the office straightening bent pipes and bending straight pipes. This was accomplished by sticking lengths of plumbing between the office wall and a fence post and by brute force and a keen eye putting in and taking out curves. For a change of pace I unscrewed rusted fittings with a sprung-jawed Stillson wrench. When in need of more violent exercise I waded into a mountain of old cast-iron gasometers with a fifteen-pound basher. Inside the meters were interesting and curious mechanical items made from brass, tin and bronze. I flattened these mysterious wheels and gears with a hammer before sorting them into piles, according to the kind of metal, for the scrap dealer.

After I had worked three weeks, we decided it was time to hit the pike again although life here was very pleasant. The bike was as good as new, and we had squirreled away twenty pounds, enough we figured to take us to Darwin. Events came to a conclusion one sunny afternoon when I was drafted into helping dig up the sidewalk over a leaking gas main. I innocently picked up a shovel used by a cantankerous old stumblebum on our digging party. This worthy commanded me to drop *HIS* shovel immediately or risk a *bash in the face*. I was astounded. Since when was touching another man's shovel a capital offence? I obediently dropped the offending tool, but mumbled something friendly, like *shove it*. That brought the stumblebum's rubby-dub mate into the fray with a virtual thesaurus of four-letter expletives. The result was a frightful ver-

Ruth, Blue, Patt and David at Rowe's Bay.

bal battle in which insults, both vulgar and picturesque, were exchanged with careless abandon. Worse, my protagonists were threatening physical violence. Having youth and a crowbar on my side, I was confident that I could give more than I would take. Fortunately, the foreman, a good-natured Yorkshire man, intervened and put a quick stop to one of the silliest altercations I have ever experienced. I told the foreman that I was leaving at the end of the week. He put me back to bashing retired gasometers. I don't care much for shovel work anyway.

In the meantime, back in camp, Ruth collected shellfish – surf clams known as *pippies* – on the beach; dug sweet potatoes in a vacant lot and shopped for tomatoes and pineapples to enhance our normal diet of steak and tea. In the afternoons there was often a *tea* with some of the wanderers who stopped at Rowe's Bay. Once a tea party was interrupted when a rather large and venomous-looking snake dropped down on the table from the overhead thatch. The ladies didn't stop to identify it. The poor reptile was bludgeoned to death on the spot.

We met some interesting people during our stay at the campground. Dennis and Asta were a couple from Sydney who, tired of the city rat race, were on their way north by motorcycle to find a new life on a far tropic shore. She was Danish, he English ex-army. Both were well endowed with the spirit of adventure. We had some fine chats over the backend billy while the Southern Cross filled the horizon.

One day a middle-aged couple arrived in a queer three-wheeled vehicle with a two-wheeled trailer attached. They were English and they had been working and wandering Australia for five years. They moved at a leisurely pace, stopping wherever seasonal work beckoned. They were full of fascinating and humorous stories but, you guessed it, they were dreadful ear bashers.

Then there was an Austrian couple who came in on a bike from Mt. Isa with a dozen two-foot-long live goannas in their saddle bags. Another biker, a Kiwi, who had travelled over most of Europe, spoke disparagingly of orthodox tourists as *Galahs*. Galahs are cockatoos that congregate in large noisy flocks.

We became friends with John, a shearer from Melbourne, who was on his way west for the wool harvest. As the wool was not yet ripe for plucking, he was having a holiday in Townsville. Later, we left Townsville and travelled as far as Julia Creek with him, bike and gear in John's Holden.

Pat and Blue, two rare characters, were roaming Australia the swagman way – hitchhiking with their scanty belongings on their backs. Pat, as you might have guessed, was Irish; Blue (everyone with red hair is called blue in Australia: don't ask me why) was a Cockney merchant seaman who, after seeing the sea from Hong Kong to Halifax, had a desire to exercise his legs on land for a change. Pat and Blue believed in camping with all the comforts of home. Whenever they stopped for a stint of casual work they visited the local dump where discarded packing cases, butter boxes and oil cans could be picked up free. These items became tables, chairs and food cupboards. Their establishment was practical and unique. One sunny day when we were having tea with the boys,

THEY TOUR TO SEE BIRDS

From
BRISBANE
May 3, 1957

David cleaning up a street in Townsville. From the
TOWNSVILLE PAPER
August 3, 1957

A YOUNG Canadian couple reached Brisbane by motorcycle yesterday to look at Queensland birds.

They are Mr. and Mrs. David Stirling, of Victoria, British Colombia, who left home a year ago.

"We got tired of waiting till I was eligible for a pension," said Mr. Stirling, 35, a former public servant. "so we packed up and left."

The Stirlings have already toured the United States and New Zealand, where they photographed birds with a 35 m.m. colour camera.

They intend to stay in Australia about a year.

Mr. Stirling said Queensland birds were well worth photographing, and "different from anything we see in North America—particularly the parrots, egrets, and ibises.

The Stirlings plan later to tour Europe. *May 3, 1957*

Mr. Stirling   Mrs. Stirling

Kindness lights the way

*sorry for this inconvenience
—we're improving your service*
Gas Company

A THOUGHTFUL apology softens the lot of Townsville (Qld.) passers-by at the gas company's repair job in the town's main street.

the conversation rounded on that favourite topic – food. After most of the conventional dishes such as roast beef and that Aussie staple, steak and eggs, were disposed of, we turned to the more exotic stuff such as frogs' legs, dugong steak and battered octopus. Suddenly Blue, who had been sitting in a pensive mood, almost shouted, "That's all very well, but I'd give it all away for a good feed of jellied eels and parsley sauce like me muvver uster mike!"

Several weeks later we met Pat and Blue again at their camp near Cloncurry in western Queensland. They had settled indefinitely into a scrap metal business with an itinerant Welshman who had given our friends a lift. Our old friends of the road invited us over to their well-furnished abode in the junk yard. Blue set fire to a pyramid of broken battery cases and bald tires. The warmth was appreciated for it was a chilly night but the greasy foul-smelling, life-threatening smoke eddying around our little party with the vagaries of the nocturnal wind, was something else. It was a grotesque and unearthly scene. The flickering flames cast eerie and fleeting bursts of light on wrecked car bodies, copper tanks, shredded tires and miscellaneous other heaps of civilisation's detritus. Overhead the wind soughed in the branches of ghostly dead gum trees; beyond in the blackness, the empty Queensland plains. The oily smoke formed a canopy, blocking out the stars. We sat facing the flames, reminiscing and sipping black tea from discoloured, chipped enamel mugs. A scene from the *Inferno*.

We enjoyed the wildlife in the Townsville area. Giant cane toads from Africa via Hawaii were a hazard. They sat, like miniature bulldogs, under the street lights, waiting to make a meal of anything from moths to scorpions. Not that they were vicious, but stepping on one of these huge amphibians in the dark was a most unpleasant form of squishiness. In the campground washrooms they were visitors to the showers and shower benches. We learned to look before sitting. Lowering your bare butt onto a large, warty toad is an experience you never want to repeat.

In a moist glade beneath spreading fig trees in the botanical gardens we found a large butterfly roost – thousands of at least ten species. They clustered along pendulous branches and created a marvellous show of colour when they flitted slowly through the sun-dappled foliage. A number ten spectacle. A butterfly roost must be seen to be believed.

From his perch on the telephone pole at our tent door, the Blue-winged Kookaburra announced the dawn with raucous laughter. Magpies joined in with their delightful carolling, and noisy Magpie-larks dropped out of the sky to drink from the dripping water tap. We heard the sweet song of the Mangrove Honey-eater only when it was not drowned out in the screeching of a hundred Sulphur-crested Cockatoos that gathered in the mango trees over at the cemetery. After a dawn chorus of screeching, the whole flock rose into the air, presenting a beautiful eye feast. Then, after several rounds of circling, swooping and screeching they settled into the trees again. As we staggered out for morning ablutions, Nankeen Kestrels and Black-shouldered Kites flew over; sometimes even a red-backed Brahminy Kite or a magnificent White-bellied Sea Eagle. The ever-present Black Kites performed their lazy circles overhead.

Black Kites congregate in spectacular numbers at the grass fires which are a common occurrence in the dry season. We counted up to five hundred swooping through the smoke and diving almost into the flames in order to snag a half-roasted lizard, rat or grasshopper. I wonder if a kite ever gets singed. Crows and Straw-necked Ibis gather at grass blazes, but they appear to forage on the scorched earth behind the fire leaving flame-swooping to the kites. When not fire-watching, kites spend their time sailing from ground level to the clouds. Reaching the top of the tower they break off in a shallow dive, slowly losing altitude, until they reach the next rising air bubble. In this way the birds stays aloft, keeping the land under scrutiny with minimum energy use, until they sight the next carrion morsel. Kite-towers add a bit of animation to a cloudless blah sky.

Birding was superb on the marshy plains and mud flats of the commonage where a host of water birds congregated. Thousands of whistling ducks preened on the sand bars. Dusky Moorhens and Eurasian Coots

A creative *Ladies* and *Gents* bathroom sign.

rotated in tight circles among the lily pads. Purple Swamp Hens were tail jerking; brilliant kingfishers eyed the shallows for minnows. Three species of sickle-billed ibis, white egrets, and quaint spoonbills occupied the swampy margins. Numerous cormorants, Australian Darters and Magpie Geese sat in meditation mode on snags and tree limbs. Sentinel Black-necked Storks stood knee-deep in the ooze, while on higher ground regiments of Masked Lapwings manoeuvred. Companies of Australian Pelicans, leisurely fishing, drifted over the lagoons while others demonstrated expert soaring in the thermals. From the plains came the stirring *giroo, giroo* of Brolgas, the Australian crane. Fascinated, we watched a mighty host of thousands performing a corroboree, their ritual dance. The Aborigines believe the cranes learned to dance from watching people.

Seeking birds in the tropics can be life threatening. One day while navigating through a tangle of burr-bearing herbs and sharp tules, attempting to get within picture range of a group of loafing spoonbills, a massive croc slid off the mud directly in our path. Fortunately for us the beast was not hungry: perhaps, it only wanted to avoid a confrontation with another vicious predatory species.

Australia's tropical north is home to two crocodile species. Johnstone's is a comparatively small, fish-eating croc that haunts fresh-water marshes and rivers. The big bad boy is the estuarine or salt water crocodile that inhabits mangrove swamps and tidal rivers. This surly reptile is capable of seizing and devouring a kangaroo or a steer and, for a change of diet, an incautious tourist. Before WW II crocodiles were numerous. Suddenly, there was an exploding world-wide demand for hides. Croc hunting became a macho *sport* and a commercial bonanza. Thousands of crocodiles finished up in shops as handbags, shoes, belts and other whatnots. In the short space of ten years, guns, harpoons and baited hooks reduced crocs to the endangered species level. Rivers still flowed to the sea and lagoons still overflowed in the Wet but the sand bars were no longer thatched with hundreds of armoured bodies basking in the tropical sun. Croc hunting was eventually banned and now these animals are common enough to be hazardous to your health again.

11

CHASING THE SUNSET

At high noon, July fifth, we drove down Flinders Street in John's Holden, heading west to new scenes. There was bitumen all the way to Charter's Towers, where we stopped to buy groceries and to view the *mulik heaps*, monuments to a gold rush of bygone days. The streets were crowded with Australian cowboys, both black and white, in high boots, riding pants and stockman's hats.

Since we carried a good water supply we were free to camp wherever a good site offered. Twenty-five miles beyond *the Towers* we brewed up and bedded down. In the morning a cacophony of Noisy Friarbirds and Australian Ravens awakened us. While we swallowed dollops of *Uncle Toby's Oats*, a mob of big grey kangaroos paid a brief visit.

The country west to the village of Prairie was a gently rolling plain broken here and there by low eroded hills covered by an open forest of eucalyptus trees that appear changeless and boring to many travellers. The discerning wanderer sees many subtle changes in the vegetation that dominates the scene. The landscape of light and airy woods is composed of waves of different species of gum trees; each kind with its own characteristics: white trunks, grey-blue shredding bark, round aspen-like leaves, grey furrowed bark, thin olive-green leaves, smooth trunks, blue leaves and so on. The species of gum tree is determined by the kind of soil: fine, ankle deep; red sandy; eroded granite with deep quartz veins; grey clay and perhaps others less noticeable. Of course if one is not interested in tree colours and soil types it looks all the same. Rivers were, at this season, rare water holes connected by long stretches of sand. These rivers must be impressive floods in the Wet. The Flinders River, where we camped one night, had water-borne debris perched high in the tree-tops. Pandanus, casuarinas and paperbarks fringing the rivers provided shelter and food for flocks of wood swallows, honey-eaters and finches.

Appropriately, at Prairie the bush gave out. A vast treeless, black soil plain waist deep in grass lay before us. Overhead, the Big Sky of Australia. It was easier to see large animals on the flat plains. Kangaroo heads frequently topped the long grass. Feral cats of the tabby variety crouched in the ditches and black razor-back hogs rooted in openings in the Mitchell's Grass. At our approach emus ran off with their feather-bouncing trot.

Hoping to get some emu pictures, we tried an old Aboriginal dodge to get the birds to come within range. The natives took advantage of the emus' curiosity by having one person wave his legs in the air while lying on his back in the tall grass. Meanwhile the rest of the hunting group, with boomerangs and spears at the ready, hid close by. The emu, for reasons known only to emus, cannot resist a pair of upside down feet. Bouncing up to investigate, the great turkey was dispatched with a flurry of throwing sticks and wooden spears. That's the story. In the interest of science we decided to give it a test. I was the leg man. With

An emu.

cameras ready, Ruth and John waited in the Holden. I pedalled furiously, encouraged by Ruth who gave a yard-by-yard commentary on the birds' approach. I thought the joke was on me when Ruth said, "We have the pictures, you can get up." I expected to see only miles of grass. Surprise! Four emus were only thirty feet away. The Aborigine hunting trick, which I thought was just another crock, actually worked.

Hughenden, Richmond and Julia Creek were typical outback towns. The first sign of human habitation was a bunch of black dots moving in the sky. Closer, these dots were identified as the ubiquitous Black Kites. The next sign was the increasing frequency of empty beer bottles and rusting tin cans. Then the dancing formless mirage astride the horizon slowly materialized into a collection of corrugated iron roofs shimmering in the heat haze. Low buildings lined the dusty streets where herds of milk goats wandered. The most important edifice in town was the pub, its bat-wing doors reminiscent of Wild West movies. Lean stockmen sat under the wide verandas gamely endeavouring to slake unquenchable thirsts while flocks of Galahs and Corellas alleviated their dry throats at the water tanks. The prevailing atmosphere seemed to be heat, dust and *to hell with it.*

Near Julia Creek we found a great blackened area extending as far as the eye could see. A fire had left only a few charred grass stems. The desolation was a great bird bazaar. Attractive pratincoles or swallow-plovers flitted about. There were immense flocks of parrots; white Corellas and pink Galahs, feeding in the scorched earth, and in flight, filling the sky. Hundreds sat on the telegraph wires. Others perched upside-down presented a curious sight. The Passenger Pigeons of America must have been like this in Audubon's day. While we watched the chattering multitudes a man drove up in a jeep, got out aimed gun and fired both barrels. Two shots, fifteen dead Corellas. We asked the reason for the slaughter. He explained that the carcasses would be laced with strychnine for fox bait. Foxes are a serious pest in these parts.

Our last camp with John was at an unnamed water hole just short of Gilliat. Driving into the bush beside the billabong, we disturbed a gathering of big water birds – pelicans, spoonbills, egrets and one darter. It was an enchanted place so we elected to spend the next day enjoying the natural history. But then we found paradise was fubar. *Homus swinus*, a worldwide species, had been here before us. Our eyes and noses soon discovered discarded smelly meat cans and broken beer bottles. Mounds of fine feathers were all that was left of plucked bustards or bush turkeys. Harmless Square-tailed Kites had been used as targets, their maggoty bodies left to befoul the air and pollute the water. It had been a fun bush camp for some sonofabitch.

The weather, muggy when we arrived, changed suddenly when a cold wind blew in from the southwest. We sat up late that night beside the roaring campfire yarning over mugs of hot tea. We awoke at dawn to a crisp cool day with a perfect blue sky – the kind of invigorating weather that comes behind a cold front. Soon the billy was on the boil and a thick mess of Uncle Toby's Oats steamed on our plates, while butcherbirds fluted in the gum trees and babblers babbled in the undergrowth.

After breakfast we reassembled our bike and gear before going fishing. The fish outsmarted us until, near give-up time, I managed to land one, a species of perch and delicious eating. When a flock of Galahs came in to drink we made dinner and watched the windrows of alto-cumulus *sheep* change from white to gold as the earth captured the sun. A nostalgic end to a perfect day.

At 10:00 a.m. the next day we had a farewell beer in Gilliat's old hotel. Then we parted company; John and his Holden south to the shearing; we and our Ariel west to whatever.

The limitless prairie changed to rougher country broken by numerous dry creek beds. The road was even rougher, and the deep sand of the creeks was treacherous for us and our overloaded bike. The cattle grids on backcountry roads were another hazard. These barriers, which hoofed animals find impossible to negotiate, are iron rail sections spaced at five-inch intervals over a wide ditch. Sometimes the grids were loose so that they moved dangerously under the vehicle's wheels: sometimes the rails have been pushed together so that there is a hole a foot or more across and twice as deep. It seemed that these barriers appeared with disconcerting suddenness in the middle of an unusually smooth, straight piece of road just as we were revelling in a nice burst of speed. Mostly we were able to screech to a stop, dismount, straighten the tracks and cross safely. Once a grid appeared just as we were wheeling along at an unusual velocity. Not only were the rails askew but there was an abrupt rise of nearly a foot in front of the hazard. I couldn't stop or even slow down. Before I could say, "Saint Christopher save us," there was a frightful crash, the shock absorbers telescoped to minimum size and we soared skyward like a ski jumper or a barn yard goose. Another spine-jarring crash indicated we had cleared the hole and were now on the other side. *Hallelujah!* We were still right-side-up and, except for a bad case of shakes, still alive.

We saw our first Ghost Gum, a beautiful white-trunked tree and our first Wedge-tailed Eagle, a huge raptor with, you guessed it, a wedge-shaped tail. We came to high fences with gates on the road. One of these was the western *dog fence*, a dingo-proof barrier running from South Australia to the Gulf of Carpentaria. The dingo, a long time ago alien dog invader, loves a rack of lamb on the hoof.

We were bowling along merrily when Ruth detected the smell of burning oil and noticed a tail of blue smoke attached to the exhaust pipe. Investigating, I found only an inch of oil remaining in the tank. A crisis. We didn't carry spare oil and worse, we were down to our last crust of bread and bit of macaroni. We would have to wait for a passing vehicle. Since we had not seen one all day it could be a long wait. Ruth, who had been scouting for signs of water while I tried to find the cause of the missing oil, came back with the good news that there was a sheep station just around the corner. Behind the grove of gum trees there was a flock of woollies drinking beside a windmill; beyond that, the tin roofs of the station. We pushed the bike up to the house where we were greeted by a burly, taciturn chap, who, when we explained our predicament and asked permission to camp overnight on his property, directed us to the shearers' huts where we had spring cots, real mattresses, carbide lights and – we couldn't believe it – showers!

Our host appeared again while we were eating our meagre supper of marmite-enhanced bread swilled down with tea. The second course, a billy of macaroni, was boiling on a small wood fire outside. He paused for a moment, and then with a look of pity or contempt, exclaimed, "Christ Almighty! Is that your supper?" He walked away and returned minutes later with two whacking great steaks the size of hand towels. We protested weakly before accepting gratefully.

When we finished our next course of prime Queensland steak with a small side of macaroni, we sat back on our cots, lit the carbide lamps and idly scanned the large selection of magazines our friend had given us. We gave solemn thanks to the stockman and Aussie hospitality. Early darkness was a good excuse for procrastination. Have a restful evening, check out the Aussie skin mags; strip the bike tomorrow.

Next morning I went to work on our rig. The sheepman, handing me a five-gallon can of oil, said, "Help yourself, mate." After some monkey wrench work and a few choice expletives I found the missing oil down in the crankcase. Dirt had plugged the oil return.

We were on the road again and into the *Curry* by noon, where we stopped to victual up and camp early at a pleasant flat overlooking the dry river where a group of transients and semi-permanent residents had set up house. Here were tents and caravans of various shapes and sizes, but one establishment was eye-catching: a complete layout of beds, tables, chairs and a refrigerator stood neatly in place beneath a spreading gum tree.

Somewhere along the west Queensland road we had another crisis: a tobacco crisis. I had kicked the habit years before but Ruth was still addicted. We had *run out*. [This old tobacco expression has almost disappeared now.] We wouldn't reach another town until next day. The situation was critical. Along the way we detoured to investigate an abandoned construction site. While we were having a leg stretch we spied a shiny round tin. It was chock full of Virginia fine cut! Crisis aborted. It seemed

SHELL TOURING SERVICE

No. 8.

TOWNSVILLE—MT. ISA — DARWIN : DISTANCE 1,640 MILES

		Inter Mileage	Total Mileage
		83	83
IX Townsville Charters Towers	Sharp turn at Mingela. Care to be exercised. Small section gravel.	67	150
IX Charters Towers Pentland	Gravel road which may or may not be. Watch corrugated. Dusty in dry weather. some for potholes. 26 creek crossings. Care to be sandy, 14 grids on this section. Care to be exercised. Dry weather road only.	96	246
I Pentland IX Torrens Ck. IX Prairie Hughenden	Black soil road with patches gravel and sand. Dry weather road only and care to be exercised 12 grids, 13 creek crossings, some sandy and steep. 1 gate which must be closed after use on this section.	75	321
IX Hughenden Richmond	Black soil road, may or may not be corrugated. 14 grids, 3 creek crossings on this section. Care to be exercised.	34	355
IX Richmond Maxwelton	Black soil road, may or may not be corrugated. Dry weather road only. 5 grids, 2 creek crossings on this section - care to be exercised.	72	427
X Maxwelton Julia Creek	Black soil road, may or may not be corrugated. Dry weather road only. 17 grids on this section. Care to be exercised.	89	516
IX Julia Creek Cloncurry	Road bad in sections, may be corrugated and potholey. Gravel road with rocky outcrops, 2 miles bitumen into Cloncurry. 15 grids, 20 creek crossings some sandy, gravel and stoney. 3 gates to be used and shut. Care to be exercised on this section. Dry weather road only.	83	599
IX Cloncurry Mt. Isa	First 25 miles wide graded gravel road, balance single track with few sections two line traffic - slow travelling. Stoney outcrops numerous creek crossings, water courses, jump-ups etc. Last 12 miles into Mt. Isa built up road. Watch for sharp gullies - care to be exercised. If travelling at night watch for cattle and kangaroos. 8 grids, 41 creek or water-course crossings, some sandy, rocky or gravel. 7 jump-ups, sharp. Care to be exercised on this section. Impassable in wet. On this section at 41½ mile peg track to left leads to Mary Kathleen Uranium Mine.		

Alternative Route — Cloncurry — Mt. Isa (Distance 143 miles)

		80	80
IX Cloncurry Duchess	Rough road with sandy patches and stoney sections. 52 creek crossings on this where care to be exercised. Impassable in wet. Dusty in dry weather.		

IX Pine Creek   65   "
IX Adelaide Rvr. 86   "

IX Adelaide Rvr. Bitumen Road
   Darwin

    The following places of interest should be seen   75   164
while in Darwin.

Nightcliffs, Mindil Beach, Botanical Gardens, Berrimah
(Qantas Terminal). Ruins of Vestey's Meat Works.

IX Hughenden   Black soil graded road, corrugates easily.
IX Winton   Travelling difficult for light cars.
   Impassable in wet.   139   139

IX Hughenden   Black soil graded road, corrugates easily.
IX Muttaburra   Impassable in wet weather.   144   14

Towns where accommodation available marked 'I'
Towns where supplies of Shell Motor Spirit and Shell
X-100 Motor Oil available marked 'X'

Happy and successful motoring is assured with the use
of this Shell Touring Service material, together with
Shell Products.

Remember, supplies of Shell Motor Spirit with I.C.A.
and Shell X-100 Motor Oil are available from all
Shell Dealers.

The Shell Co. of Aust. Ltd.,
301 Ann Street,
BRISBANE.

24/11

A sample from the
SHELL TOURING SERVICE
Brisbane, Australia

that the gods, perhaps, in the case of tobacco, the demons, were with us. Well, it is always good to maintain cordial relations with both groups.

From Cloncurry to Mary Kathleen, the road was under construction. For bike riders the conditions were frightful. Miles of deep, crushed rock with pointed edges alternated with miles of deep dust. Adding to the general unpleasantness were herds of bulldozers and other earth-moving machines the size of dinosaurs. Worst of all were the non-stop gravel trucks. Coming upon us from both front and rear, in dust as thick as a brick wall, these leviathans held the course down the centre. We were forced to hug the treacherous verge, bouncing crazily over the boulders and ruts while dodging showers of missiles fired at us. Struggling to keep bike upright, I was sweating like a bull moose in fly season. We were caked with dirt beyond recognition. (Read the *Shell Touring Service* road report again on pages 106 and 107.)

Mary Kathleen. This company town's sole reason for existing, plumb in the centre of the wilderness, is the rich uranium ore, waiting to be separated from Mother Earth. We gave the town a quick *once over* and moved on.

The road from Mary K. to Mt. Isa was, if possible, worse than that to Cloncurry, with one exception: no traffic. At a pleasant water hole we made camp, scraped, beat and washed off some of the case-hardened dirt before settling down to the inevitable mugs of hot tea. All around lay eroded, stony hills covered with a thin forest of scrubby trees. Between the rocks were rounded clumps of that vegetable hedgehog, the spinifex. I climbed one of these sun-blasted rock heaps, where from the summit I had a magnificent panorama of this *empty* wilderness. What colours the low sun painted this austere country! What a change from the drab blaze of high noon! The crumbling rock was now a potpourri of the surreal art of creation. Grey-green mounds of spinifex wandered over the broken earth beneath the gnarled white trunks of ghost gums. The hills rolled away wave upon wave to the deep purple eastern horizon. When the sun dropped below the edge of the world the entire western sky instantly turned red. In this picture the planet Venus gleamed suddenly.

A sample of the road across Queensland.

Overhead, thin mare's tails invisible in day-light materialized in pure gold. From the east the twilight curtain, sharply defined in this crisp atmosphere and spangled with stars, rushed up as the Earth rolled into its own shadow. It must have been a mind-blowing scene like this (minus spinifex and gum trees) that inspired Moses on Mt. Sinai to chisel out the Ten Commandments.

Early next morning while slowly manoeuvring our trail through rocks and dust, we were nearly turned into a large Frisbee by an unexpected Volkswagen moving at excessive speed. Then another vehicle hotly pursued by yet another emerged from the dust storm. Ahead, a straight piece of trail was just an elongated wall of dust. Still more vehicles coming. We quickly went into a *get the hell off the trail mode* and started counting. Twenty-seven cars passed. For some time dust merged earth and sky into one. It was the *Around Australia Ampol Oil Trial.*

In the mining town of Mt. Isa we stopped for some shopping as there were only two victualling points between Isa and Tennant Creek: the small town of Camooweal, a hundred and twenty miles west, and a store with a petrol pump at Frewena, two hundred and eleven miles beyond Camooweal. A good bitumen highway began at Mt. Isa, stretching with only a few curves westward for four hundred miles to the join the Stuart Highway north of Tennant Creek. Like Mary K., Mt. Isa sits fair and square in the heart of the sunburned wilderness.

We found a windmill and made a comfortable camp in a nearby dry creek bed. We were tired after battling the rocky road to Mt. Isa and driving into the sun on the shimmering black asphalt. In the silent night we heard the Stone Curlews wailing, *Wee-loo, wee-loo* – eerie and wild, far away on the dark plains. We were on the Barkly Tablelands, a vast, almost treeless plain extending from Queensland to the middle of the Northern Territory. This low plateau is covered with lush grass that springs up during the short rainy season. Surface water is almost non-existent. This is stock country, made possible only by bores: deep wells drilled at intervals across the entire region. At some bores, water gushes to the surface unaided but mostly windmills do the job. Bore water in its long stay below ground is *hard* with dissolved minerals and often hot, but it is *wet* and that is the main consideration in a thirsty land.

Windmills are a most welcome sight in the Outback. A windmill means water. In the evening all creatures great and small gather for the daily tank-up at the bore. Cattle, sheep and horses, the reason for the well, come in herds and droves. Swift flocks of parrots, bounding kangaroos and long-striding emus approach at dusk. Around the bore the earth is strewn with the bones of the departed. Animals, sick and aged, prefer death with a belly full of water. For people too, the windmill visible from miles away, is an overnight stop.

Near Sudan Station, we camped one night where the Rankine River provided an extensive, though muddy, water hole. It was a fine site with shade trees, dry wood, soft sand for comfort and plenty of water. We had our tea then idly strolled along the river enjoying the abundant pandanus trees. Galahs in tens, hundreds and thousands were arriving from every point on the compass. They were not coming for just an evening drink. They were going to stay the night, and we were camped right under their roosting trees. We got precious little sleep that night with ten thousand parrots talking in high screaming voices directly above our tent. It was worse than trying to sleep under a cocktail party table. And no mitigating vodka. The birds were bad enough but the multitude of tiny red ants that surfaced to feed on the parrot droppings that fell like intermittent rain, was even worse. Our tent, recently fitted out with floor and mosquito bar, did not deter those little red boogers. Fortunately, the ants didn't bite but their infernal crawling nearly drove us round the bend. Saint Vitus's dance with ants. There was more. A stiff southerly gale at midnight dislodged branch loads of our feathered bed partners, causing them to make one hell of a racket. At dawn the huge wheeling flocks of Galahs were a magnificent and colourful sight but our bloodshot eyes could not do justice to the spectacle.

We met Scotty, a lone motorcycle wanderer off to Darwin after a successful year's employment in the Mt. Isa mines. He wanted to tag along with us even though we warned him that we were in no rush. For us it was the journey not the destination that mattered. We wanted to view the landscape, gaze at the sky, watch birds and enjoy everything the wild Earth had to offer. Scotty was a raw-beetroot vegetarian, a flaming communist, a zealous proselytiser and a disciple of the Red Dean of Canterbury. He was a crusading idealist who needed a sounding board for his endless lecturing about the coming Brave New World. His was a religion based on people on the ground instead of the old sky stuff, but with the same old intolerance. In other words, he was a monumental ear basher and a proper pain in the butt. Waving his arms in a three hundred and sixty degree circle, Scotty would say in a voice dripping with emotion, "It's a shame; it's criminal, that this empty land is not open to the starving multitudes." Empty land? That is the charm of this country. Empty land? The land is not *empty*. It is full to carrying capacity with kangaroos, wallabies, termites, parrots and ants. Should these creatures

Termite skyscrapers are BIG.

be replaced by a teeming load of humanity? Well, that was my position. And this land had a serious water shortage.

Of course Scotty was not alone in this thinking. Canberra-bound senators and trough-bound Ottawa bureaucrats are always advocating blooming deserts and populated polar ice fields, before drinking a large glass of cool water and high-tailing it back to their comfortable homes in more congenial climes. Once a wild-eyed J. W. collared me (for only a minute) to tell me about his dream of multitudes living high on manna from Heaven in Antarctica.

In Scotty's brave new world ruled by wise, honest bureaucrats [an oxymoron], war, taxes, poverty, jails and all the other ills that have afflicted mankind ever since history was written and even before, would be remembered only in history books. Of course, history must be rewritten. People of this Utopia would be free from all the usual vices and obey the Ten Commandments and the Golden Rule without blinking an eye.

At first we had discussions, then discussions degenerated into arguments; finally my retort to Scotty's endless lectures was only a rude but emphatic, *bollix* or *bullshit*. We parted company amicably in Darwin.

He: "Enjoy Darwin," meaning, "Some day when I am commissar...."

Me: "Enjoy your ride south" meaning, "Up your kilt with a wire brush."

One evening Scotty's tedious droning was interrupted by the damnedest noise imaginable. It was a two-syllable gurgling gasp repeated half a dozen times. The creature sounding off seemed to be just outside the circle of our campfire light. During the night we heard the noise close to our tent. In the morning we set out to try to discover the source. The strange calls sounded again from behind a low hill. Peering cautiously around the knoll we saw a small meadow and a smaller water hole. The Bunyip we expected to see had vanished. Not a sign of life. The mystery was not solved until weeks later. At the government farm at Berimah, near Darwin, I heard those raucous calls again. I asked one of the workers if he could enlighten me regarding the music.

"That's a jackass," he said. "The country is swarming with them." We had been fooled by a serenading feral ass. At that time we didn't know the Australian bush was *swarming* with donkeys gone wild.

We expected to find tropical forests in the Northern Territory, similar to those of north Queensland but the country was a limitless plain broken here and there by low ridges and rocky outcrops. At Katherine we found the first river with running water, not just sand and a few water holes. This was the Katherine River, a tributary of the Daly. The lagoon near Dunmara was a splendid bird city. Water birds galore! Australian Pelicans, spoonbills, egrets, Brolgas, Glossy and Straw-necked Ibis, Masked Plovers, Pied Stilts, White-necked Herons, Pink-eared and whistling ducks. And land birds! Red-tailed Black Cockatoos, Galahs, Peaceful Doves, Crested Pigeons, Magpie-larks, crows, kites and harriers. Some species were present in huge flocks. We made rough but conservative estimates of twenty thousand wood swallows and twenty thousand Budgerigars. A birder's vision of paradise.

We had some excitement that night at Dunmara. We should have known better as we considered ourselves experienced bush persons. We had extended one of the tent's guy cords across an animal runway. In the blackness a feral boar trotting to the lagoon caught its leg in the rope and wrecked the tent. Only the anchor of our sleeping bodies prevented pig with tent attached disappearing into the bush. A two-foot-long gash on one side necessitating an immediate tedious mending chore while a mob of mosquitoes gave us their undivided attention.

When the World was created, God gave northern Australia to the termites with the command: go forth, multiply and build clay skyscrapers. The termites went into building on a vast scale. The diversity of size, shape and colour is truly astonishing. In places the mounds were the size, shape and colour of tomb stones; vast cemeteries extending for miles. There were fairy-tale castles: low flat-topped mounds with numerous turrets and spires projecting heavenward. This type was common on fine sandy soil. Another kind was four to five feet in height, thicker in the middle than at the base, cone shaped on top, with a few flanges sticking out at various points. These, found in circles and clumps of a dozen to several hundred, were usually brick red in colour. Once we saw twenty of these in a circle around a large Ghost Gum. In the twilight the view was startling. It looked like a group of monks in long robes with heads bowed in prayer around a sacred tree. A shrine of nature worship in the silent bush. Magnetic termite castles are special. These, about five feet tall, are lens shaped with the narrow edges facing north and south. This construction presents maximum surface to the sun. The

A Ghost Gum tree.

tallest structures we saw were north of Katherine near Darwin. One was over sixteen feet from ground to top and roughly circular with a turreted penthouse crown. Termite houses are hard as concrete but break off easily at ground level. Unfortunately, this weakness has given rise to the outdoor sport of *bashing* [pushing over] *ant hills.*

Termite hills are both living quarters and food storage bins – like the now rare and endangered Saskatchewan grain elevator. Millions of chambers inside the tower are storage bins for seeds, grass stems and other minced vegetation. The whole is kept at a constant temperature and humidity. This original air conditioning is necessary not only to prevent food spoilage but also for the health of the little beasties, for termites are intolerant of extreme weather changes; even strong direct sunlight can kill them. The latter fact I saw for myself while working at the forest nursery near Darwin. There, termites and I were in a constant state of war. I noticed that a box of tree seedlings was getting ravished. I moved the box and found a whole village of termites underneath. Within a few minutes the termites, exposed to the noon blaze, were turning belly up. Before all could succumb, the ever-present bull ants moved in and carried off, to their underground lairs, the warm and still kicking bodies.

One might liken the termite colonies to ancient city states and the bull ants to tribes of semi-nomadic barbarians. A sealed termite city is an impregnable fortress. Only during construction or when winged males and females are being hustled out are there openings to the outside world. Even then the open galleries are plugged by hard-headed soldiers with mandibles like twin scythes. The bull ant's chance comes when a tower is damaged or overturned by a falling tree, an itchy water buffalo or a playful person. The termite soldiers, invincible in the static defence of narrow alleys where each battle is fought according to the book, are hopelessly outmanoeuvred by the blitzkrieg of the ants. The panic-stricken workers are carried off quickly for they know nothing of this kind of warfare. The soldiers are dispatched by the simple tactic of attack from the rear. The sluggish creatures, invincible in frontal assault, are grabbed by their backsides and hauled away to the ant's larder.

The most important event in the life of a termite colony takes place on a humid overcast day in the rainy season. A million winged kings and a smaller but numerous bunch of queens set off on brief aerial honeymoons before dropping back to earth to found another city. Gangs of workers open passages on the tower's roof. Soldiers stand guard ready to repel invaders. In the chambers below the surface other workers are grooming and marshalling the nobility for their big day. Then, when all is ready, the cream of the crop is launched to ensure that termites will not perish from the earth. Many are out of the race quickly for they are feeble, bungling astronauts. Hundreds crash into tree branches and grass stems and into the jaws of waiting ants. Others fly into webs cunningly constructed in the line of flight by bloated spiders. Those that escape these hazards have to evade the hosts of birds that have gathered especially for this event. In the trees, honeyeaters, rollers, flycatchers and bee-eaters have a banquet. In the air, flocks of black curved-winged swifts, patrolling beneath the rain clouds, catch the high fliers. Termite colonies are maintained only by prodigious production. Perhaps only one queen in a million lives to carry on the termite line, but a host of other creatures are assured of full stomachs when the termites fly.

12

FLAMING FURIES AND MINDIL BEACH

Viewed on a map at the other end of the world, Darwin seemed to be a fabulous place. In 1957, seen at close range on the ground it was disappointing. Although the small downtown area was clean and modern (for the1950s), the approaches were marred by miles of rusted Nissan huts, mounds of dead beer bottles and partly constructed shanties. Sunken ships lay in the harbour. The ships were reminders of Japanese bombs; the empties were monuments to the thirst of the thousands of Australian and American soldiers who passed through here on their way to bloody battlefields farther north.

Unless you were a visiting government official or a person of independent means you headed for Mindil Beach, where squatters rights prevailed, find a shady tree and set up housekeeping. In those days Mindil Beach, where we lived for six months, was home to a remarkable cross-section of the world's societies. There seemed to be few if any rules except for some unwritten ones created by the residents themselves.

At the bottom of the heap were the no-hopers, usually married, with a bevy of small children. No-hopers were invariably booze artists. From Friday night to Monday morning the environment was loud and hideous with the drunken caterwauling of beach party attendees. Parties usually produced at least one good fight accompanied by picturesque and original language. The unmistakeable sound of falling carcasses among beer bottles and packing case furniture marked the termination of the argument. It is only right to note that some weekend party persons were *respectable* people from town, not beach residents. The extent of boozing at Mindil was phenomenal. We thought we had fallen in with Alcoholics Unanimous.

Domestic arguments were another feature of beach life. I remember a marathon row that started at 10:00 p.m., kept me awake most of the night, and was still raging at 6:00 a.m. next day. The unfortunate part of it was although the nattering was severe enough to keep me awake it was not clear enough to let me follow the entire novel. From the bits I heard I am sure it was a blockbuster.

Of course the beach population was not totally made up of no-hopers; on the contrary these people were in the minority. Nevertheless, in any community they make a splash far out of proportion to their numbers.

Most of the residents on the beach were solid citizens, pillars of the church and the PTA, who finding a place free from land taxes, and having settled into permanent work, had swallowed the anchor – whatever term is applied to sedentary caravanites. Their caravans [trailers] had been jacked up, and in many cases add-ons and small gardens of bananas and papayas completed the domestic picture.

Many of the beach people were nomadic workers seeking the big money construction jobs; adventurers, stopping on their journeys around the world, and Australia tourists from the southern cities. There was a bunch of world travellers with original methods of transportation. An English couple from London had come across Eurasia by motor scooter with sidecar attached. Two Italian men were on their way around the world on state-of-the-art motorcycles. A Canadian couple with a beat-up Fordson van was *doing* Australia. Two English couples on motorbikes were waiting for a ship to Singapore. A German had canoed to Darwin and was having a rest before the next leg via the Pacific Islands to the Americas. Another young German chap, an unrepentant Nazi and a racist of the old school, was a frequent visitor to our camp. He dismissed Aborigines as *stupid*; Italians and Russians as having *no education*. He had spent his Boy Scout days with the Hitler Youth and at war's end was with the army retreating through the Carpathian Mountains with the Soviet troops chewing at their heels. He was a good story teller. We had some lively arguments.

With more than three hundred people squatting on Mindil Beach, sanitation was a problem. There was a brace of water taps where the inhabitants could exchange gossip while filling dixies and water bags, and a pair of corrugated iron shower chambers that were sometimes messed up by dogs and people. The most important facility was several batteries of *flaming furies*. In the absence of sewers and septic tanks, the flaming furies took the place of the old-fashioned outhouses with crescent-slotted doors. In corrugated iron sheds a half-dozen forty-five-gallon oil drums were buried with about two feet sticking up above the ground. Crude wooden seats were placed on top of the open drums. Each fury battery except one had doorless booths allowing for a slight bit of privacy. One of these sheds had no divisions; just a friendly row of six black drums where neighbours could sit and chat while answering the calls of nature. *The family fury*.

And now the reason for the name. As you can imagine, smell and flies were something to cope with. Twice a week the sanitation crew from town made their rounds with used oil and packing case wood. This mixture was dumped into each drum and set alight. Result: a column of evil, black, oily smoke that on calm evenings formed a canopy over the beach. The aroma would drive a dog off a gut wagon. This treatment masked the stink for a day or two and distressed the flies but failed to lower the drum's contents by an appreciable amount.

A quick check of our financial state showed we had six pounds Australian, six dollars American and one dollar Canadian. It was not the time to ponder old clichés such as: *It's only money*. Only said by those who have it to burn. *Money doesn't bring happiness*. It brings something so close you can't tell the difference. *Money is the root of all evil*. We must go for a chunk of that evil root. Now! Two days job hunting – no luck. Then, just as we were looking wistfully at and caressing the last pound note, I secured a pick-shovel-pneumatic drill job with Australian Blue Metal.

I was one of a small crew levelling a site for a quarry and rock-crushing machinery. In any part of the world this would have been manual labour; under the molten sky of Darwin it was hell. Only the well-patronized water bags hanging on strategic trees around the area prevented total collapse. I drank and sweated, sweated and drank until ten days later I felt and looked like a boiling water bag myself. I estimated I was drinking four gallons of liquid in the form of water, tea and a ration of one bottle of beer each day. Ninety-eight percent of this was returned to the atmosphere in the form of sweat, only two percent was reached the ground as pee. Well, I might be exaggerating a bit, but I think these figures were pretty close. When I was labouring, head down butt up, I had visions of a cool pub with foaming glasses of brew approaching on an endless belt. All I had to do was hoist each glass as it reached me. Sometimes I heard Paul Robeson singing, *"Darkies All Work on the Mississippi."* In Darwin roles were reversed, white folks worked while the dark folks meditated and played their didgeridoos in the shade, beneath the gum trees. Domesticated Aborigines were common in and around Darwin, converted by pious missionaries to the true faith, tobacco and plonk. *Wild* people sometimes wandered in from Arnhem Land and the deserts of the south-west carrying long spears and wearing only tattered shorts or even just birthday suits.

In the comparative coolness of the early morning, before my eyes were blinded by sweat, I saw some new birds. Large, slow-flapping Red-tailed Black Cockatoos, usually in groups of threes, flew over. Butcher birds and Blue-winged Kookaburras perched above us watching our activities with cheerful indifference. My greatest bird thrill came one morning while gathering dry wood for the billy fire. (I had been promoted to *smok-o man*, a position of highest priority for the morale of the crew.) Right under my nose was the bower of the Great Bowerbird. Although I had seen a pair of these birds at our diggings I had not expected to see a bower so close to the work site.

The bower was on a bare patch of earth close to a small green shrub. Made of tightly woven twigs, it was twelve inches high by eighteen inches long. The twigs were bent so that they formed an arch; on the bottom they formed a meshed floor. At either entrance, extending out about two feet, there was a fan-shaped carpet of rock pieces picked up at our quarry. Bits of clear glass and the bleached shells of giant land snails were scattered over both fans. In the centre of the bower there was a *nest* of fragments of clear glass and perfect snail shells. The interior walls were covered with a thin coat of grey clay. The artist had painted each twig with a solution made from rock dust and saliva. Naturalists who have seen the bird at work have reported that it often uses a brush made from shredded bark.

During our levelling operations a tree was accidentally felled on the bowerbird's playground. The feathered craftsman began construction on another bower immediately, only four feet from the original. The old bower was left intact except for the snail shells and bits of glass, the most prized possessions. The new playground was a replica of the old except that some brightly-coloured berries and leaves were added.

All of Australia's eight species of bowerbirds build playgrounds, bowers or mounds of one kind or another. The shining blue Satin Bowerbird

Patio and bower of the Great Bower Bird.

prefers blue objects for decorations. Discarded Reckitt's bluing bags are one of its prized acquisitions.

The dry season concentration of birds at Humpty Doo was spectacular. On a visit to the paddy fields in early August we were overwhelmed by numbers and variety. Birds: Straw-necked and Glossy Ibis, Pied and

White-necked Herons, Royal and Yellow-billed Spoonbills, Brolgas, Jacanas, egrets, ducks, pratincoles. Most abundant of all were the big black and white Magpie Geese. And lots of smaller stuff too: Magpie Larks, Australian Bee-eaters, corellas, kites and harriers. A staggering wildlife spectacle.

At that time an ambitious rice growing project was earmarked for the low plains of Humpty Doo and Marakia. The Australian government and a private company were already into it, but Magpie Geese were converting the season's harvest into goose grease and guano. For geese, concentrated domestic rice is preferable to tough native grasses and roots. There was talk of wholesale poisoning. A quick fix, too late for this season, was an army of shotgun toters, to blast the varmints back into the swamps. Hungry people must be fed, not geese; progress must not be delayed.

We were just settling in on Mindil Beach when four dusty chaps in a dustier Land Rover braked to a sudden halt beside our tent. We were pleasantly surprised to see the faces of Dennis, Ray, Ron and Keith materialize from behind their dirty masks. Five months ago, on a picnic with them in the Blue Mountains, we learned that they were on the road to Darwin via Alice Springs. We had been on the road via the east coast and north Queensland for five months. They had reached Darwin by way of the interior. We all arrived in Darwin only twelve hours apart.

The arrival of Dennis and his *cobbers* was our good fortune. In less than a week they were all gainfully employed with accommodation! We fell heir to their luxurious camping gear. We now possessed a large tent with fly, a card table, two stools, a hurricane lamp, a Morris Minor bucket seat and sundry other small items including a mysterious, fancy chamber pot that the boys had discovered amongst their gear when making camp in the southern desert. Or so they said. We were moving up. We now had the pot but still no window to throw it out.

We set about making a comfortable permanent residence. Under a shady tree we pitched the tent on a floor of packing-case wood liberated from the flaming furies wood pile. I felled some wattle poles with my machete, scrounged some burlap sacking and nails, borrowed a hammer and presto, twin cots. Orange boxes with centre partitions became cupboards and book shelves. Light from the hurricane lamp hanging on a wire from the ridgepole was a luxury.

The living room-dining room was a flimsy wall-less structure of wattle poles held together by a tarpaulin roof. Roll-down burlap blinds were added for shade and rain brakes. One saddlebag, the food pack, hanging by a thin wire well above the ground was our larder. A solid pile of flat rocks and an iron grill was our outdoor kitchen range and barbecue. Upturned tea chests beside the fireplace provided counter space for cutting, and storage space for pot and pans including the mother of all cookware, a huge, black cast-iron kettle, known as a camp oven. A genuine witch's cauldron.

Things were definitely looking up. Ruth obtained one pound a day for a three-hour cleaning job at a tourist guest house. Just as I was on the verge of being reduced to a small grease blob at the Blue Metal quarry I was saved by the Forestry Department. I was now in charge of the forest nursery at the Berimah Experimental Farm. The forestry staff consisted of the chief forester, the boss, me, nursery i/c and my assistant, Michael, a mission-educated native from Melville Island.

The native forest at the top end of the Northern Territory is a wooded savannah made up mostly of Eucalyptus species reaching seventy to eighty feet in height. The trees look healthy but many have been reduced to hollow shells by termite and rot. The hollow trees provided homes for forest denizens from bees and reptiles to birds and beasts, but to the commercial forester they were junk to be replaced with plantations of fast-growing softwoods.

Throughout this open forest grew scattered fan palms and pandanus. The forest floor was covered with tall grass, herbs, wild grape and palm-like cycads. While wandering in the bush at the height of the dry season we found two very unusual shrubs. One was a low bush with numerous thick up-swept branches like a stag's antlers in the velvet. Not a leaf on the plant, only three or four rose pink morning-glory-like flowers adorned the bare stems. It looked like someone had decided to add some colour to the drab scene by sticking a few flowers on a dead tree. Bush number two was just a slender pole, usually on a slant and possessing a few short twigs on which clusters of yellow blossoms hung. Both plants seemed out of place, even artificial.

The Forestry Department was anxious to establish fast-growing pine plantations in the tropics similar to those solid areas of *Pinus radiata* so noticeable down south. I planted seeds of *taeda, longifolia, radiate, halepensis* and *patula*. Although pines had priority, I cultivated Mexican Cedar, Florida Cypress and Indian Teak. As a *hobby* I planted a few seeds of lemon, mango, date palm and coffee. Nursery work consisted mostly of planting seeds and caring for the seedlings of tropical and semi-tropical trees from warm countries around the world. Keeping the delicate seedlings moist and happy was a chore, as this was the peak of the hot, dry season. I set seeds in boxes and tubes under shade or covered the beds with straw and watered three times a day. But even this was a problem as the main pipe lay uncovered on the ground exposed to the direct rays, bringing the life-giving liquid's temperature to near the boiling point.

Insects and fungi regarded the nursery as a welcome feeding station. Here was water and a tasty array of tender seedlings and nourishing seeds. Termites topped the list of unwanted visitors. They ate their way along the tree roots and into wooden boxes unnoticed until the tree wilted and died or the box and its contents collapsed like the *one horse shay*. Next in the line-up was a tiny red ant, a terror on seeds. The first signs of its depredation were neat lines of granulated soil corresponding exactly to the seed rows. An entire seedbed might be cleaned out overnight. And then there was *damping off* caused by a fungus, *fusarium*, the nemesis of tender, baby plants. The only way to keep ahead of the enemy was eternal vigilance, and, only as a last resort, doses of insecticide and fungicide.

Other insects and their relatives were numerous. Ant lion pits encircled the bases of trees, harvesting surplus ants. A large, colourful, thin-waisted mud dauber wasp was a frequent visitor to the dripping water tap while several other kinds of parasitic wasps patrolled the ground in their nervous manner. I saw a small beet-red wasp dragging a praying mantis twice its size into a previously dug burrow. A giant grasshopper that could leap ten feet with ease was common. The spider tribe was, as usual, well represented. Hairy wolf spiders lurked under the always present corrugated iron sheets; funnel-web spiders built their silken tunnels in the hardest ground; hairless, poisonous red-backs dwelt in most cracks and crannies.

Food was a bit of a problem. Fruit and vegetables came north from South Australia by rail to Alice Springs, by truck from Alice to Larrimah and then by rail again to Darwin. No wonder apricots were selling for six shillings a pound. Local beef, at a reasonable two shillings was excellent for a long session of jaw exercise. *Air beef* from Alice was tender but at seven shillings was *treat meat*. Dried fruit and cereals were often infested with weevils. It was easy enough picking the little black buggers out of the rice but de-weeviling the raisins was something else. Milk, in three varieties: condensed, evaporated, dehydrated; no fresh.

In addition to the road-rail service from Adelaide and Alice Springs there was coastal shipping from Perth and an occasional boat from Sydney via Cape York. The sea route was favoured for heavy construction materials and non-perishable food stuff. During our sojourn in Darwin there was some strife on the wharf. It seemed that the wharfies, Australian stevedores, were on the verge of striking at regular intervals, especially if there were more than two boats in the harbour. There was a story, perhaps true, that a strike had been called but within a few days there was a major crisis. The beer supply ran out. Throats parched, bodies drying out. Fortunately, a shipload of Swan Lager arrived from Perth. Strike suspended, booze unloaded, strike resumed. Stevedoring in Darwin was a tough job.

I obtained a limited quantity of fresh vegetables from the experimental farm in August and September but the increasing heat signed finis to the temperate crops. In October the pineapples and mangoes were ripe. Pineapple became daily fare. The huge spreading mango trees were

Snowstorm To End Tonight; Cold Staying Over Weekend

Alberta's early-October snowstorm, one of the worst on record, is expected to end tonight, but the cold weather is predicted to last through the weekend.

So far, the storm has left seven inches of snow on the ground in the Edmonton area, while in the Grande Prairie area, there is 18 inches on the ground. A forestry station near Jasper reports 37 inches on the ground—at Jasper town there is just a skiff of snow.

The weekend forecast issued Saturday by the weather office, called for cloudy, cold weather, with intermittent snow ending Saturday evening. Winds during the day were expected to be northwest at 20, dropping to light in the evening. Low temperature overnight is expected to be 15, with a high Sunday of 30. Winds Sunday are expected to be 10 to 15 m.p.h.

For the football game at Clarke Stadium Saturday night, the weatherman predicts 10 to 15 m.p.h. winds, no falling snow, and a temperature in the low 20's.

The three-day storm, termed by weather officials "one of the worst on record," has halted harvesting indefinitely, plugged roads, and disrupted transportation and communication. It reached the blizzard stage in some districts.

The snowfall at Edmonton is 8½ inches, with seven inches still on the ground. Peace hold reports seven inches on the ground, Lac la Biche nine inches, White Court, eight inches, Grande Prairie 18 inches, with a recorded snowfall of 22 inches; Banff, six inches on the ground; one foothill forestry station reports 24 inches on the ground, another, 37 inches.

(Continued On Page 2, Col. 5)

SNOW? WHAT'S THAT? — Palms and fields of sugar cane drowse peacefully in the sunlight on the outskirts of Edmonton. Before rushing off to see their eye doctors, however, Edmontonians should be informed that this is Edmonton, Australia, not Edmonton, Alberta. Mr. and Mrs. David Stirling, former residents of the Edmonton (Alberta) district, sent the photo from Darwin, Australia, where they are now basking in the summer heat.

From the
EDMONTON JOURNAL
(CANADA)
Saturday, October 3, 1957

loaded. In order to get our share of the fruit before all was devoured by bandicoots, flying foxes and others, I climbed into a fine fruity tree and from my airy perch I snared mangoes with a wire loop attached to a long pole. Ruth, on the ground, caught the projectiles in order to prevent loss and damage. All was going according to plan until Ruth, blinded by the sun, was hit on the forehead by a stone-hard, kidney-shaped fruit. She fell stunned. I dropped the pole and started down, but I was gripped by red hot fire from bare feet to hat. I had blundered into the leafy nest of the green tree ants. I had to endure the stabs of hundreds of burning needles until I hit the good earth and flung off shirt, shorts and underwear. No more mango gathering today.

A few days after this episode Ruth developed a nasty rash. The fiery bloom started around her mouth and quickly spread over her face and even to her arms and legs. At the hospital the doctor said, "Allergy."

While we are revelling in the mango glut we were also experiencing a caterpillar *plague*. One morning thousands of small white sausages began lowering themselves, on silken ropes, from our tree. When they reached the ground or our hair they began spinning their cocoons. Loopers were everywhere: our food, our beds, our hair and even in the clothes on our backs. It was a number ten larvae spectacle. When the air drop ceased, ten days later our home site was swarming with little blue butterflies.

Was the allergy the result of exposure to caterpillars or was it the result of overindulgence in mangoes? Ruth stopped eating mangoes. The rash died down and soon disappeared. Was it mango or butterfly larvae? That was soon solved when Ruth started eating mangoes again and sure enough the rash came back. Mangoes taboo; leaving more fruit for the flying foxes.

Flying foxes are mega fruit-eating bats with fox-like faces and wing spans of four feet. A special flying mammal. We saw them for the first time at Cairns where hundreds flew across the twilight glow every evening. Their slow, flapping flight was more like that of large herons; not swift and fluttering like smaller insectivorous bats. We thought they were herons at first sight, flying to roost, not mammals heading out to find dinner. During the day flying foxes hang out in large *camps*. Camps may roost several hundred individuals. We found such an aggregation in a dense forest patch at Howard Springs. We heard their noisy bickering before we saw them, for like many gregarious animals they are exceedingly quarrelsome. The treetops were hanging with big fellows. Some were fanning themselves with membranous wings, others clambered about in a grotesque manner. Most seemed bad-tempered and irritable, trying to oust neighbours from their favourite perches while constantly shrieking. It was like eavesdropping on a pacifists' convention.

There was at that time a huge weathered edifice known as Vestey's Meat Works. It was constructed in the late 1930s but was never used because WW II intervened. Some government vehicles were stored in one of the large killing rooms, and a few squatters had set up housekeeping in other parts. But most of the gloomy vaults had been commandeered by bats, of the small insectivorous kind, for dry roosts.

When we saw streams of bats issuing forth from Vestey's just as the sun dropped into the Timor Sea, we decided to have a closer look. Without using a torch we slipped in quietly. While gingerly feeling our way into the room we sensed the presence of strange creatures. Perhaps it was the subdued rustling and the nose-wrinkling smell, or perhaps it was the Stygian blackness or perhaps it was all of the above that generated an overall creepy feeling. My tattered sandal made contact with something that after a brief resistance burst like a ripe apple. I flicked on the torch. The floor was wall-to-wall black cockroaches the size of baby turtles. Except for waving their antennae, they squatted immobile on the floor vibrating their palpi and watching us with ruby red eyes. Between the cockroaches the guano floor was heaving with maggoty crawlers; walls were thick with hairy wolf spiders.

We didn't want to upset the scene but where were the bats? We shone the torch onto the ceiling of the next vault. It was a solid mass of small bats all neatly crowded together like sardines in a can. All the bats took wing simultaneously. The room was thick with flying furry bodies. Naked wings brushed our faces. The bat-generated wind stirred up a powerful smell of guano, rot and ammonia. We shut off the torch and stood quietly. The bats returned to roost. When the commotion ceased we sneaked out. We were looking for a false vampire or ghost bat, a pallid, carnivorous species that captures smaller bats on the wing, but no luck. In nature's economy every species is food for another. Bats in the Vestey.

The northwest coast of Australia has one of the greatest tidal ranges in the world. The maximum range at Darwin is about thirty feet. At low water spring tide, the sea retreated to the horizon leaving a world of sand and mud exposed. It looked like you could walk dry shod to Timor. Twice a month the sea swept into the flats and mangroves beside our tent like a river in flood bringing new life to the molluscs and crabs that survived the dry times in burrows and under mangrove roots. One of these survivors was the amphibious bug-eyed mud skipper. We often saw them perched on tree roots several inches above a muddy pool. Beche-de-mere, a species of large, purple sea cucumber, was numerous enough to maintain a chain of Chinese restaurants. With the tidal flood came clattering hordes of hermit crabs, with borrowed shells of different colours and sizes, marching inland to forage. We found some of these little explorers a quarter of a mile from the beach.

An enjoyable feature of the Timor shore was the sea on the *door step*. The daily swim was memorable but that was about to change. In the Dry, when winds and currants were offshore, seaborne nasties retreated north. In the morning, bathing was delightful; in the late afternoon the water coming in over the scorching sand was too hot for comfort. The salt content was very high because of the action of the overhead sun on the shallow sea. In late October our bank account had shot up to two hundred pounds. The Wet was on its way south, bringing with it deadly stingers such as sea wasps and the Portuguese-man-of-war. Warnings arrived via the radio and press. But there was only one near-fatal bathing incident during our stay in Darwin and it could not be blamed on nature's beasts. A moron in a power-boat ran over a young airman.

We moved our bathing activities to Berry Springs, a fine fresh-water hole, except on Sunday afternoons when the crowds from Darwin marred the ambience. Among the Sunday visitors there seemed to be a rather high percentage of yahoos who enjoyed the sport of tossing beer bottles into the pond and firing .22 rifles at both dead and alive targets.

Another of our leisure activities was the Tuesday evening visit to Darwin's small but excellent library. It was a cool (temperature) place and the ice-water fountain was a mouth-drooling luxury. Our special sections were wildlife, botany, tropical agriculture and tropical diseases. Speaking of diseases: too much eye contact with the colour plates in Manson's *Tropical Diseases* was guaranteed to produce nightmares for weeks. Our morbid fascination was intensified by Ruth's mango rash, eruptions of tropical ulcers, the results of sandfly bites, and my bout with tropical ears, a fungus infection, contacted, perhaps, from bathing in the old swimming hole. In reality, northern Australia is mostly free of the many diseases so common in other tropical countries, but there was an outbreak of Dengue, a mosquito-borne disease. I asked a Mindil Beach resident, "What are the symptoms of Dengue?" His reply, "You'll know it, mate. You'll think your ahs-hole has dropped out."

13

THE WET

The sun rose higher, the heat got hotter, the southeast trade winds dropped to an airless calm, broken occasionally by hard, swirling bursts from any quarter bringing intense but brief dust devils. The mercury got stuck in the high 90s F. Inland, great anvil clouds mushroomed into a sky of molten brass above the shimmering grey bush. At day's end we biked out to the high ground at Nightcliffs, to enjoy the sunset. The sun, blood red from the smoke of bush fires and pockmarked by sun spots, seemed to hang motionless for a moment before plunging into the Timor Sea. A terrific sizzling noise and a cloud of steam would not have been a surprise. Crepuscular rays shot up from sun's bed. Sea, sky and clouds turned to pink and gold. With darkness, continuous lightning played around the southern horizon, illuminating the distant boiling thunderheads. For a storm watcher it was magnificent. The monsoon was just over the horizon.

The stratosphere-punching cauliflower columns were at the mercy of the fickle breezes that broke the oppressive calm most mornings and evenings. The land breeze of night produced, by morning, massive clouds over the sea and clear skies over the land. The deluge seemed imminent. Nothing happened. By smok-o the great clouds were barely mole hills. By noon, only blue sky over the sea. Now, a light but refreshing on-shore breeze took command, building towering thunderheads over the land that in turn disappeared with the contrary winds of night. One day the sea breeze was stronger and did not give way to the nightly land breeze. A great current of humid air moving down from the equator had given a kick in the rear to the local winds. The Wet had arrived.

The thunderheads grew until the sky could hold no more; lightning joined clouds and ground; violent downdrafts sent termite-riddled trees crashing to earth. Then rain – not gentle rain, but violent suffocating rain – rain that did not penetrate the baked ground, but instead, covered the flat land inches deep and rolled off in flash floods down the gullies. Local clouds, brewing up fast, frequently destroyed themselves with a crashing downpour.

A swift change came over the Earth. The monotonous sameness of the Dry was replaced by the dynamic instability of the Wet. There was new living energy in the air. Frogs, surveying the world from their homes in knotholes, croaked a deafening welcome to the rain, before hopping away to ancestral breeding puddles. Mindil Beach residents now had to battle mosquitoes and other insects that increased a thousand fold overnight. The vegetation shot up so fast that some plants didn't appear to have a young stage. Dry clumps of grass merged into waving waist-high acres of green. Everything that was not treated to a daily airing sprouted a sheen of mould.

A remarkable change came over the birdlife too. In the up-drafts, just ahead of the rolling squall clouds, hundreds of sickle-winged swifts gyrated, their wild *scree-scree* calls in keeping with the awesome turmoil in the sky. The Koel, a large blue-black member of the cuckoo tribe; the Dollar Bird, a roller, and the beautiful fat Nutmeg Pigeon (Pied Imperial-Pigeon) returned from spending the dry season in Indonesia. A pair of nutmegs set up house-keeping in our shade tree and repeated non-stop *ook!-whuu.* Brilliant lorikeets, rosellas, fig-birds, Yellow Orioles and honeyeaters became abundant with the appearance of new blossoms. A Pheasant Coucal sat in the pandanus trees venting a loud *coop-coop.* The spectacular dry-season concentrations of water birds began to break up as they scattered to breed in the new wetlands. Shore birds arrived, riding the north wind from their summer breeding grounds on the Siberian tundra. Some only lingered for a day or two before drifting off farther south. Largest of the lot was the Far Eastern Curlew. Whimbrels, another of the curlew family, were common along the shore. The third species, the Little Curlew, arrived *en masse.* One morning I watched hundreds materializing from out a particularly black storm front, dropping to the grass and standing motionless as if exhausted. How far had they flown? Two days later they had all moved on. Pacific Golden Plovers, Terek Sandpipers, Greenshanks, godwits and Marsh Sandpipers were some of the many Eurasian migrants that stopped or passed through. In the short evenings we biked out to check for the latest bird arrivals and watch the sunsets from Nightcliffs. Here be Grey-Tailed and Wandering Tattlers on the rocks, a row of Brown Boobies roosting on an old pier cable, and a pair of ubiquitous Ospreys at their nest on a disused pylon.

The dawn bird chorus changed. Not much in the realm of song but the melancholy *hooting* of the Pied Imperial Pigeon, *cooing* of the Peaceful Dove, *cooping* of the Pheasant Coucal and the *cooeeing* of the Koel combined to make a pleasant bush symphony. We missed the mass twittering of a thousand wood swallows that greeted sun-up in The Dry. Absent too, was Jacky Winter, the chanting flycatcher that entertained us with a twenty-minute recital every morning: *Tuitty fruity, tuitty fruity, what's your beer, tuitty, fruity,* plus at least ten more phrases that I can't translate into English.

14

BIRDS AND BEASTS BESIDE THE TIMOR SEA

We slipped into the routine of eight to four with free weekends. The experimental farm workers and I were picked up each morning by covered truck and transported to our labours thirty miles south. We were a taciturn lot. Only John greeted the gang as he climbed over the tailgate. "Gentlemen of the jury," he sang out with a smile. It never varied; always, "Gentlemen of the jury." Response was a boorish grunt or two. Sometimes I said, "Good morning, John," just to make him feel good and to ensure that he would say "Gentlemen of the jury" again next day.

Sport shootin was a favourite outdoor activity in the Northern Territory. Using kangaroos, wallabies, emus and water buffaloes for targets can hardly be called hunting or even *sport*. Survey gangs, geophysical crews and tourists were all well-armed and too often used their weapons indiscriminately. New European immigrants seemed to be the worst offenders. In Europe, hunting opportunities and guns were restricted; in Australia the frontier mentality still prevailed. While roaming the bush we often saw families of red wallabies watching us from only twenty yards away. We saw water buffaloes so close we thought they were barn doors. Pointing a loaded gun at any of these animals hardly required skill or courage. But mankind has been a slaughter-happy animal ever since he discovered the lethal pointed stick.

The water buffalo was introduced to Australia from Java back in the early gold rush days. Gone feral, they are now *thick* as water buffaloes can be in the wetlands of the north. Since buffaloes was not native they were outside the game laws. Off and on there have been local meat and hide industries but they didn't prevail. Massive horns make fine trophies for people whose egos require nourishment from the sight of a dead animal staring down from the wall. Buffalo meat was extensively used in bush camps. Once we were presented with a chunk. It fitted our witch's cauldron nicely and became a tasty stew. We heard rumours of a massive government extermination campaign being considered for sometime in the future.

The goanna, a large, swift creature, is the feature lizard of the northern bush. We found three species, although we had no lizard field guide. There was the water monitor, which was our swimming pool companion; the lace monitor, a slim fellow that could vanish up a tree before you could say *go anna*; and a big terrestrial chap four or five feet long, the scaly king of the bush. A lace monitor, about two-and-one-half feet long, was a daily visitor to the forest nursery. It wandered about as if it owned the place. It was there first. After I offered it a grasshopper on the end of a short stick it became a friend. It was a master of the disappearing act. One day I watched it start its glide up to the trunk of a gum tree then move around to the other side. I moved to the other side too, expecting to see my reptile on its way up. But it had vanished. All I could see was

Home sweet home, Mindil Beach.

a perfectly smooth bole for thirty feet with no visible branches or holes. The big chap, the bush master, relies on camouflage for protection. It will flatten its body on the ground until the enemy is close enough for a tail grab. This is the method used by the Aborigines for procuring dinner. "It tastes just like chicken," said an Aboriginal chef.

One day we observed a great commotion in the avian world. Rollers, honeyeaters, swifts and pratincoles were converging on a particular spot in the bush. Investigating, we found a stream of flying ants. A colony of bull ants was sending out its winged males and females. Birds were gathering for a high cholesterol feast. Moving into the centre of the action I nearly stepped on a pair of goannas tonguing up the goodies. The lizards charged for cover, each in different directions. One entered a hollow stump only a hundred paces away. I wandered over to have a look and found a situation rather common in the animal world; the goanna was well hidden except for a foot of protruding scaly tail. Why don't we pull it out, observe it at close quarters and take some photos? Why do we think like that? Why can't we just leave the animals alone?

I attached a rope noose to a pole and secured the protruding tail. I tried to pull him out but he wasn't for it. I didn't want to hurt the beast but I was determined to outwit him. I tightened the pull then relaxed several times, then a mighty surprise heave. He or she was out. I had proved that man's cunning was superior to a reptile's. The goanna was four feet long and of course it made a frightful commotion before being safely deposited in a gunny sack.

We incarcerated the goanna in a hastily-constructed but roomy cage for a couple of days. I don't know why, other than we wanted to observe it and get pictures. If it got friendly it could be released to roam around the vicinity of our abode. It spent hours on its hind legs, front claws hooked in the cage wire, gazing wistfully at the green outdoors. We could stand it no longer. We opened the cage. After a moment's hesitation the lonesome beast scuttled off to the uncertainties of freedom.

We had more than our share of small lizards. They often glided over our bare feet while we ate our meals. We amused ourselves and befriended the animals by feeding them captured horse flies. Geckos, small fly-catching lizards, were everywhere including inside houses. They appear at night usually close to a light source where moths and other insects accumulate. They blend so well with their environment that only their *tok-tok-tok* calls give them away. While sleeping on the ground one night covered with only a sheet, I felt something clammy moving over my back. I lay still, trying to conjure up a plan of action. The *thing* kept moving and seemed to be several feet long. Seizing the sheet and the unknown species I hurled both as far as possible. Grabbing torch and machete I prepared for battle with, perhaps, a death adder. It was only a large skink, a cold, damp reptile that lives under rotten logs. Because it has weak legs it propels itself in the manner of a snake.

Perhaps the most unusual Australian reptile and the one guaranteed to make a stalwart dipsomaniac sign the pledge, is the frilled lizard, an animal almost two feet long with a nine-inch neck ruff. This bizarre creature is a champion bluffer. When threatened it instantly extends its frill, and opens its bright yellow, cavernous mouth showing a pair of nasty looking teeth. This display is accompanied by a loud hissing. If bluff is of no avail the dragon retreats swiftly, running upright on its hind legs.

We heard plenty of wild snake stories before we arrived in Australia. To venture beyond the pavement without knee-high snake boots and a snake-bite kit was suicide. Although we ignored these exaggerations we always treated snakes as venomous unless proven otherwise. And we had a snake bite kit. We avoided prowling around in high grass and swamp margins at night and gathering firewood after dark. Australia does have more than its share of snakes, well beyond a hundred species. Five of them: taipan, tiger, black, death adder and brown snake are highly venomous and should not be messed with. The black snake and the brown snake are common and may be aggressive if threatened. These two are responsible for most of Australia's snakebites. The death adder, a fat, sluggish reptile inhabiting rocky country, only bites if kicked by a hiker, but then using its tail spine for purchase, it hangs on and chews.

Several species of non-venomous pythons are fairly common in the north. They are often encouraged to hang around farm buildings because of their appetite for rats. At Mindil Beach a young camper had a friendly pet, a black-headed rock python which could be handled with impunity.

In a land where snakes are numerous, non-venomous species are disadvantaged. If a snake underfoot appears aggressive do you have time to identify it or can you leaf through your snake field guide? Most times it is shoot first and identify later. A snake slithered across Ruth's feet while she sat reading at the beach. It headed for the tent. She attempted to head it off with a piece of firewood. Snake reared up in fighting mode. It was dispatched with a smart bash. We never got its name. While building our *humpy,* my peripheral vision picked up a small snake about to make a grab for my naked big toe. Instinctively I dropped my hammer with considerable force on its head. This specimen was identified later as a usually harmless kind, only slightly venomous. I had no desire to test it on my toe. Perhaps it was only having a look at what could be a fat slug. Snakes are supposed to thrash around before giving up, not until sundown according to the old snake lore, but this one didn't even twitch.

In late December the next phase of the monsoon took over. Low ragged clouds were blowing in with the steady northwest trade wind. Gone were the fascinating electrical storms of the beginning of the Wet. The temperature, lower by a couple of degrees, was preferable to the Turkish bath atmosphere of November. Flocks of tiny, gaudily garbed finches flew in to devour the ripening grass seeds. The finches landed on the seed heads, bore them down and promptly vanished from sight in the thick vegetation. Frogs croaked joyfully everywhere. Hordes of mosquitoes took advantage of the overcast days to work overtime.

In the height of the monsoon we were left homeless. Dennis and the boys arrived with the news that they were off to Sydney via Queensland. Their tent and gear that had made life so comfortable and pleasant was going with them. The solution to our housing dilemma was: build a *humpy* quick. I rode in sheets of corrugated iron on my bike from Vestey's, a rather dangerous venture but fortunately completed without mishap. Some wattle poles, a dozen rusty nails and presto, a rainproof abode with twin bunks. It was comfortable in a relative sort of way, and it fitted in nicely with the beach décor. Keeping up with the Joneses was not a problem on Mindil Beach.

Ruth quit her job at the guest house and went to work at the Kool-Bar Café, the only quick food establishment in town and the only eatery that stayed open until after the grog shops closed at 10:00 p.m. It was, as you can imagine, very popular with the drinking crowd. It was a rough place, but the pay of seventeen pounds ten shillings a week was almost as good as winning the Golden Casket, the Aussie sweepstake. Perhaps

Drifting and dreaming.

tips too. We had dreams of a bank account soaring high like swifts and kites in the monsoon sky.

Ruth's first evening at the Kool-Bar was easy: if washing dishes is better than dealing with the mob of raucous, intoxicated humanity that charged in at ten. By the end of the week she was able to deal with every species of drunk and to remember every complex food order that was hurled at her. The tough New Australian Greek boss had the right personality for preventing his boozy customers from annoying his three-waitress staff, and every night there were four cool quarts of Swan Lager in the fridge to keep boss and employees hydrated.

The pleasant, cloudy weather of the Wet was marred by the super-abundance of flies – house, blow and several others – that took the joy out of eating outside. The aroma of grub, especially meat, was a signal for a buzzing multitude to attack. Flies were not welcome at the dinner table anytime but when you are aware that between meals they were visiting the Flaming Furies it was disgusting.

Christmas morning: jingle bells and Ho! Ho! Ho! Santa arrived at Mindil, shouting, "Merry Christmas, you bastards." He was in full beard and red costume, sitting on an easy chair in the back of a Holden pick-up truck. In the humid heat he must have been sweating bottles of ink. He moved slowly along the beach repeating his greetings. I am not sure if he was *official* or just some joker from the beach folk? Either way it was a good start for Christmas Day.

Later, the day was noteworthy for continuous rain and a dinner di-saster. We bought a choice roast of beef Christmas evening, wrapped it in several layers of paper and cloth and hung it in the food pack where we thought it would be well armoured against the bluebottles. Christ-mas Day we readied the camp oven, carefully unwrapped the non-turkey treat and behold, a seething mass of robust maggots. The bluebottles had triumphed. We were dumfounded, depressed and thoroughly pissed-off. Maggots develop fast but given the time involved this piece of meat must have been blown before it was secured, perhaps in the shop. After a ceremonial burial of the moving dinner, we had a melancholy non-feast of canned sardines, tinned plum pudding and tea. Then we repaired to the humpy to be entertained by the drumming of rain on the iron roof and, to enhance the melancholy mood, eye-ball the colour illustrations in *Manson's Tropical Diseases*.

The no-hopers were in the throes of a series of memorable parties from this side of Christmas to the other side of New Year. Outdoor tables were sway-backed from cases of beer and flagons of plonk. Parties in relays. In vino, talk (loud), gossip, argument, jokes and cursing (foul). One bunch was sleeping it off while others celebrated in raucous fash-ion. During these days an hour's peace and quietness was almost inde-

A typical 'Humpy'.

cent. Since this was love-thy-neighbour week there was only one row but it was noteworthy. My father once remarked that when he was a young soldier in Ireland, you could get a glass of beer and a black eye for four pence, and if you weren't satisfied you could get another black eye for nothing. It was much the same at Mindil except there was one important difference: a glass of beer was a shilling.

New Year's Day brought a remarkable change in the weather. The sky was blue and cloudless, a refreshing breeze blew up from the south, the temperature dropped ten degrees; the nights were almost chilly. It felt like a feast of pheasant and champagne after months on bread and water. In midsummer, a huge cold front bursting out from the icebound continent of Antarctica had brought snow to the hills of Tasmania, frosts in the state of Victoria, and rain to the interior deserts. At Darwin, only twelve degrees south of the equator, it had reversed the northwest monsoon at the height of the rainy season. The part played by the Antarctic frigid air dome, even in the tropics, is truly astonishing.

The brief interlude of dry cooler weather helped to bring our sojourn in Darwin to an end. We were thinking about heading south anyway as we had, by spending almost zero, amassed a fortune of five hundred pounds Australian.

Mike and I had planted a lot of seedlings in the grassy bush beyond the nursery fence. A mistake. Even now, in the Wet, there were clumps of dry stuff about. On the weekend a wandering party of wild men, on seeing a goanna or some similar critter snaking for cover, had fired the grass and wiped out our plantings and the nursery. On Monday morning I viewed a scene of desolation. Smouldering posts hung on the fence wires and the new seedbeds were trampled beyond recognition. Months of labour had literally gone up in smoke. Mike had gone home for the holidays. Two days later the chief forester returned from another seed collecting trip. Needless to say he nearly had a stroke and a heart attack in the first minute. He would issue me a .45 automatic. My orders: shoot anyone coming within range of the plantation. Later, when we and the fence posts had cooled down somewhat, my boss admitted that this was not the answer and might even be illegal. He was short of funds and, perhaps, it might be better to start a forest plantation at a more secure site. After all we were sitting on a traditional walkabout route. He was relieved when I said we were thinking seriously of moving on. He said he needed to get away for long vacation too. I had thought he was always on holiday.

How would we travel to Adelaide? It was the worse season for the two-thousand-mile journey via Alice Springs to Port Augusta, the port of Adelaide. The desert south of Alice would be a waterless inferno. We didn't feel up to it. Working in the heat and humidity had left us thin and weak. I felt and looked like an underexposed negative. Ruth said I looked like a walking Adam's apple.

15

WITH BEER KEGS AND BARBED WIRE TO ALICE

We decided to ride out on Outback Transport, the weekly truck service, to Alice Springs. From Alice we would ride the Ghan south. We thought the rail journey would be a welcome and restful change from bike and tent. The company would deliver our motorcycle and camping gear promptly to Port Augusta for the sum of seventeen pounds ten shillings.

Before pushing off we were guests of a charming New Zealand couple. We found a house stay a pleasant luxury after months of natural living on the beach.

We left Darwin several days ahead of the truck in the vain hope that we could hitchhike to Alice thereby saving the five pounds per person the company charged. We hated to part with any of our hard-earned stake, and we were thoroughly conditioned to living on next door to nothing. We had no trouble getting rides the two hundred miles to Katherine but that was the end of the line. In those days nobody was going south. Not one vehicle was venturing beyond Katherine. For three long days we waited beneath the almost-no-shade of a thin-leaved, small ironwood tree, the only tree available, moving around a step ahead of the sun. Sharing the scant shade was a young English couple who had bussed, walked and hitchhiked from London via Turkey and Afghanistan. Their daily struggles and closeness of months on the road had left them rather tense. They weren't speaking to each other. On the second day two young fellows who were out to see Australia on the cheap joined us, and then three Christian Brothers appeared. It was a good lesson in overpopulation: the mercury nudging the 110 degree Fahrenheit mark; the sun a couple of notches north of straight up; nine bodies competing for a few square feet of partial shade. Too many people for a scant resource; a microcosm of the world.

On the third day the brothers had a private prayer session. We hoped they were asking for an early arrival of the transport, but all we got that night was a heavy downpour and hordes of mosquitoes. Nine bods made a fast exodus to the nearby post-office veranda where we endured an awful night swatting insects and constantly turning our numb and sleepless carcasses on the hard boards.

As dawn broke we heard the welcome roar of an approaching diesel. Praise the Lord! Perhaps prayers had brought deliverance after all. Outback Transport was here at last. We grabbed our sleeping bags and rushed to get on board the big open-deck semi-trailer. Even the brothers were in a state of panic. Being left behind for another week of togetherness under the ironwood tree was too much to imagine.

Each one of us tried to find a little space of our own in the cargo of beer kegs, oil drums, rolls of barbed wire and other items of assorted hardware. Our bike was not among the stuff. We rearranged the cargo somewhat and rigged up a small tarpaulin as a sun-wind block. Only a short distance into the journey we realized that the super hot wind was our worst enemy. Exposure to the on-rushing, searing air would turn us into beef jerky before we reached Alice.

An endless shimmering ribbon of macadam stretched south under a scorching sky. Talk soon became desultory and finally ceased. The engine's roar was a lullaby to us sleep-deprived passengers. The country became drier. Gone was the tall grass of the north. From Daly Waters south, the country was arid but even here spaced acacia and gum trees gave the land an airy forested appearance. The driver made frequent stops and detours to unload and pick up various items. All day and all night we pressed on until at daybreak next day we stopped for a hearty breakfast and a much-needed loo break at the mining town of Tennant Creek. What a relief it was to eat, stretch and perform the necessities.

Here, we first encountered the desert flies, small replicas of the house fly. They were out for moisture, sweat and other bodily fluids. These insufferable insects swarmed over any exposed body part, probing into cuts, sores, mouth, eyes, nose holes and ear holes without even a preliminary buzz. Flapping, waving and swatting only seemed to attract them. Perhaps all this exercise just produced more moisture. The best plan was to try to ignore them, but this was not easy when a fly slurped in each eye corner and another just traded a stranger's nose for your mouth.

Nearing Alice Springs the scenery changed. We were passing through the Macdonnell Ranges. Purple mesas on the horizon, red sandstone bluffs near the road and dry, stony creeks lined with silky casuarinas and beautiful ghost gums. An ancient land that had remained the same for ages yet had seen many changes wrought by wind and water. A harsh but beautiful land. The setting sun painted the wilderness in colours of purple, red and gold. This was the country of famous Aboriginal artist Albert Namatjira. His paintings capture the pure beauty of the land.

It was a relief to climb off the truck, collect our packs, pay the driver his ten pounds and shuffle off with numb legs and stiff backs to the nearest café. We had travelled nine hundred hot, sometimes dusty, very uncomfortable miles in forty hours in an open truck with seven other sweaty bodies and a load of assorted freight.

In the relative cool of the café we consumed the biggest possible order of steak and eggs washed down with double milkshakes. After six months on rough tucker in Darwin, Alice was paradise. The next two days were noteworthy for feasting on fruit and fresh milk plus of course the inevitable steak and eggs.

Today, it seems like everyone is attached to a backpack – school kids, tourists, wanderers, business blokes. In 1958 it was a rare sight. Two woebegone travelers under large packs was a recipe for a few long stares from the good citizens of Alice. In fact, we wondered, who were those two persons gazing back at us from shop windows?

With Ann and Tony, the English couple, we looked for accommodation. Ann and Tony, scraping the bottom of the money barrel, suggested trying the Salvation Army. We were not happy about this as we felt we would be taking advantage of these good people and perhaps sneaking beds away from other more deserving persons. At the Sally Ann two severe-looking women appeared positively happy to see us. Business was slack. There wasn't even a drunk body on the floor. As we had our own bedding, all we needed was four canvas cots under a roof. It was the most comfortable home we had had for more than a week. On leaving, two days later, we slipped a small donation into the charity box. The initial wave of guilt was assuaged.

When not eating and resting in the shade we wandered the town seeing the sights: the John Flynn (the famous flying doctor) Memorial Church and the dry Todd River fringed with robust white-trunked gum trees. At sundown, we climbed Monument Hill where we had a fine panorama of Alice Springs, a green oasis, beneath the purple Macdonnell Ranges.

16

THE GHAN

We climbed aboard the Ghan with our packs *tied* to our backs as the Australian magazine, *Woman's Day*, reported. The trip south was a pleasant adventure. Berths were comfortable, food was good. The Ghan rarely hit top velocity of thirty miles per hour as the tracks were laid on the desert without ballast. An excellent speed for landscape gazing and wildlife watching. The journey to Adelaide takes three days if all goes well. At Christmas, the train was held up for two weeks because the Finke River, swollen with unusually heavy rains, burst its banks.

South of Alice we swayed through inhospitable desert and then the strange Gibber Plains, a vast pavement of rocks polished smooth by sand driven by the south-west winds of winter. No vegetation, only *gibbers*.

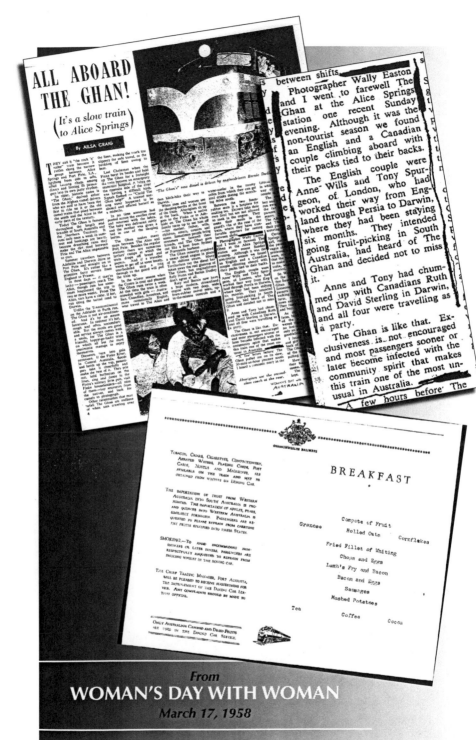

ALL ABOARD THE GHAN!

(It's a slow train to Alice Springs)

By AILSA CRAIG

The "Ghan's" new diesel is drawn by enginedrivers Bernie Dudd...

Aborigines use the second class coach at the rear...

WOMAN'S DAY with...
AUSTRALIA...

between shifts.

Photographer Wally Easton and I went to farewell The Ghan at the Alice Springs station one recent Sunday evening. Although it was the non-tourist season we found an English and a Canadian couple climbing aboard with their packs tied to their backs.

The English couple were Anne Wills and Tony Spurgeon, of London, who had worked their way from England through Persia to Darwin, where they had been staying six months. They intended going fruit-picking in South Australia, had heard of The Ghan and decided not to miss it.

Anne and Tony had chummed up with Canadians Ruth and David Sterling in Darwin, and all four were travelling as a party.

The Ghan is like that. Exclusiveness is not encouraged and most passengers sooner or later become infected with the community spirit that makes this train one of the most unusual in Australia. The

A few hours before The

BREAKFAST

Compote of Fruit

Granose   Rolled Oats   Cornflakes

Fried Fillet of Whiting

Chops and Eggs

Lamb's Fry and Bacon

Bacon and Eggs

Sausages

Mashed Potatoes

Tea   Coffee   Cocoa

COMMONWEALTH RAILWAYS

TOBACCO, CIGARS, CIGARETTES, CONFECTIONERY, AERATED WATERS, PLAYING CARDS, POST CARDS, NOVELS AND MAGAZINES, ARE AVAILABLE ON THE TRAIN AND MAY BE OBTAINED FROM WAITERS ON DINING CAR.

THE IMPORTATION OF FRUIT FROM WESTERN AUSTRALIA INTO SOUTH AUSTRALIA IS PROHIBITED. THE IMPORTATION OF APPLES, PEARS, AND QUINCES INTO WESTERN AUSTRALIA IS SIMILARLY FORBIDDEN. PASSENGERS ARE REQUESTED TO PLEASE REFRAIN FROM CARRYING THE FRUITS SPECIFIED INTO THESE STATES.

SMOKING.—TO AVOID INCOMMODING NON-SMOKERS OR LATER DINERS, PASSENGERS ARE RESPECTFULLY REQUESTED TO REFRAIN FROM SMOKING WHILST IN THE DINING CAR.

THE CHIEF TRAFFIC MANAGER, PORT AUGUSTA, WILL BE PLEASED TO RECEIVE SUGGESTIONS FOR THE IMPROVEMENT OF THE DINING CAR SERVICE. ANY COMPLAINTS SHOULD BE MADE TO THAT OFFICIAL.

ONLY AUSTRALIAN CANNED AND DRIED FRUITS ARE USED IN THE DINING CAR SERVICE.

From
WOMAN'S DAY WITH WOMAN
March 17, 1958

South, beyond Oodnadatta, there were small patches and lines of ghost gums, desert willows and saltbush fringing bald knolls or framing dry watercourses. In the Lake Eyre region we saw shimmering white lakes of salt and clumps of strange vegetation. Everywhere we saw the wages of dehydration – piles of bleached animal bones and mummified carcasses.

Australians have solved the problem of keeping dry throats moist along the desert railway line – build a pub at every remote station. When the Ghan slowed to a walking pace approaching a stop, long-legged ramblers deboarded, sprinted for the watering hole and were already choking down the first pint before the train stopped. When the Ghan pulled out the rehydrated passengers, with a quart bottle in each hand, ran alongside catching the train on the fly. One bottle was passed to a friend on board leaving the other hand free for grappling the iron horse. Later the tickling of broken glass was added to the music of the rails as dead soldiers were fired out the windows.

About three a.m. on our last day, we entered a powerful electrical storm with continuous lightning and heavy rain. A crazy Hungarian, who shared our compartment, and who was suffering from a chronic case of Soviet Tankitis, an epidemic raging in central Europe at that time, insisted on switching on the lights and shouting in a frightened voice, "Big light, plenty light." And other picturesque words we couldn't figure out but which sounded like good old spectacular cursing and blasphemy. In vain we tried to calm him with soothing words such as, "It's only nature getting rid of surplus electricity; shut up and let us get some sleep." We thought a Russian invasion of central Australia was unlikely at that time, but the poor devil carried on his scary monologue until we passed out of the storm. It was most annoying. He must have had some terrible experiences before escaping to Australia.

Under stormy skies daylight crept in over the Flinders Ranges. There must have been more rain here. Cows, sheep and horses began to take shape in a landscape that was almost green. As light increased we began to see wildlife. Kangaroos, sitting on their fat tails, watched the train rumbling through their domain. Emus were common in pairs and bands

The entire population turned out to welcome the Ghan.

of up to eight or ten. If disturbed near the rails these big birds shuffled off only a few yards with their peculiar gait, then turned and stared. There was plenty of smaller stuff too – crows, Galahs, Budgerigars and Magpies. But the most interesting of all was the Wedge-tailed Eagle, remarkably abundant here. Perched on the overland telegraph poles or soaring in wide sweeps they were a picture of avian majesty.

We arrived in Port Augusta at eleven a.m. after the best morning of wildlife viewing and the inevitable massive breakfast of bacon and eggs. No sign of our bike. After enquiries at the depot and a telegram to Darwin, which was never answered, we decided to cadge our way to Melbourne via the thumb method. We were not amused. It was a major disappointment as we were looking forward to a long, leisurely bike and tenting trip via Tailem Bend to the Coorong, an eighty-mile lagoon crammed with birds, mallee trees and sand dunes, and a stop at Mt. Gambier's famous blue lake.

Three days and several mostly uneventful lifts we arrived in Melbourne. Only one ride was different and a bit scary. We were picked up by two young Aussies who drank steadily from a never-ending supply of quart bottles. They were good talkers. The driver, with one hand on the wheel, the other for delivering a swig to his mouth from a tightly clutched bottle, was perched at a forty-five degree angle on his seat so that he could look us back seat passengers in the eye while rambling on. Somewhere near Ballarat, as night was closing in, the boys said they knew of an inexpensive hotel. It looked like a burned-out hulk, and it was. A caretaker emerged from the charcoal and said there were several unburned rooms that had never been slept in. They were available at the bargain price of five pounds per room. He winked slyly and said he would have the water and lights on for a half hour but we must keep the blinds closed. It was all hush-hush. He was pocketing a few quid to augment his caretaker's pay.

What to do? We were miles from the main road, a light rain was falling and it was coal-mine dark. Let's go for it. We moved in past the charred frames that we hoped would hold the building up until we got away in the morning, and inspected our room. The smell of ancient grease, burnt meat and charcoal was overpowering, but the beds had clean sheets that appeared to be pristine although having a full ashtray aroma. It was a relief to get on the road next morning.

17

BEANS, PENGUINS AND A KOOKABURRA

At Melbourne we contacted Peter and Margaret, who had settled there. They donated their floor for sleeping purposes. We spent the next two weeks in this fine city doing the tourist thing: visiting Saint Kilda's Road, botanical gardens, Olympic swimming pool, war memorial, and of course Phar Lap the famous race horse in the national museum and Chloe the equally famous nude painting in Young and Jackson's pub. We looked up John, our sheep-shearing cobber from Queensland days, now back home in Melbourne after a successful season. We spent a nostalgic evening reminiscing while enjoying his mother's home-cooked dinner.

We booked our passage to Southampton on the *Castel Felice*, which was leaving Melbourne on April 8. For the fare of one hundred and fifty pounds each we would be in two separate rooms each with six persons of the same sex and well below the water line. This was not a problem. The *Castel Felice* was a one-class ship of the Italian Sitmar Line. Except for sleeping, we would spend the voyage of forty days and nine port stops above decks as we had the run of the whole ship.

We had six weeks until departure. Perhaps we should look for some casual farm labour again. We heard the usual tales of fortunes to be made grape picking in the Mildura wine country and hop harvesting in Wangaratta. Both places were miles away and we had no transportation. Our bike had disappeared. Then in Friday's paper we saw: *Bean pickers wanted*, at Silvan, only thirty miles away. After some enquiries we gathered that the financial reward from bean picking was considerably below that of grapes or hops. And even worse, bean pickers were considered to be at the bottom of the farm labour strata. Nevertheless, we would give it a go.

Monday morning, a forlorn last call to the depot. Strike me pink! Praise the Lord! Our bike was waiting! It's incredible! We had given up hope. I hustled down to the depot for a joyful reunion. One can get emotionally attached to one's wheels. We phoned the farm to explain that we would be a day late as we needed another day to do some minor repairs and sort out our gear. There was some visible evidence that our rig had been ridden around Darwin for a couple of weeks. Perhaps just paranoia?

We arrived at the farm just as a fierce thunder storm brought early darkness. Fortunately, before we got soaked we were directed to a hut containing two bunks, a table, a couple of chairs and a fireplace.

Next morning at eight we were introduced to the back-busting job of bean harvesting. Pay: it is piecework; ten shillings for a fifty-pound bag. It sounded OK at first, but when we had filled one sack we found we couldn't straighten up. Muscles had become so stretched that they refused to contract. We were faced with the horrible prospect of spending our remaining years shuffling about on all fours – a case of reverse evolution. We decided that high-balling was silly. Better take it easy until we got used to the new posture. We soon established a norm of from four to seven bags a day depending on our mood and the state of the bean patch. We were slightly ahead of the worst pickers, but far behind a husband-wife team known as the *gun couple*. *Gun* being a prefix describing a person who, with skill and determination, exceeds all others in contract labour – a Free World Stakhanovite.

I suppose you could call the bean picking bunch a *weird mob*. Tony, the wog, worked an eight-hour night shift in a jam factory, and then put in nine hours in the bean patch. He sometimes dropped dead between the rows for a half hour's catnap. One day he left at noon never to return. I hope he made enough money to establish his own restaurant or bakery. Elmer, a tall blonde youth, was a real oddball. Extremely taciturn, his stock expressions were only *yuh* or *nuh*. If he had any knowledge about anything he didn't spread it around. He had the reputation of being a kleptomaniac. Chet, an ex-Indian army chap, had many interesting stories to tell, but he always punctuated his conversation with a liberal sprinkling of Hindustani. Ron, who lived with his ancient mother, was an exquisite cook and preserver of fruit. He spent his Sundays up to his wrists in pickles, chutneys, jams and jellies. He loved to talk recipes and was very generous with his creations. His reputation suffered somewhat when at the bottom of one of his jam gifts we spooned out a huge wad of chewing gum complete with teeth tracks. Lucky we didn't get mum's false teeth too.

A sad-eyed Irishman, from the Green Glens of Antrim, and a rather large blond woman, know as *the old lady*, lived next door to our home. Drink was Paddy's downfall. He frequently begged off work on Friday afternoon to go into town *on business*. He showed up in the bean field on Monday morning, his eyes like two poached eggs in a pool of blood, sadder but apparently no wiser.

We settled into a pleasant routine. Good outdoor labour. When the beans were off there were strawberries to pick, when the strawberries were finished there were lemons to harvest. A lemon day was as good as a rest, because we could stand up on our hind legs, normal human posture. The kookaburra's laughter at dawn was our alarm clock. Eating was good. The butcher, the baker and the milkman made their weekly rounds. Our boss was generous with the farm's fruit and vegetables provided we weren't flogging his produce to the city folk that drove past. He said that this was not uncommon.

Peter and Margaret spent a weekend with us. Our living quarters were cramped, but we had a jolly time fishing in the dam, hiking in the in the sunny woods and birdwatching. Margaret, who had become a keen birder, was intrigued by the many blue wrens and honeyeaters on the property. We found a colony of Bell Miners in the wattles by the creek. After an active day in the sun we sat down to a bang-up dinner of prime Aussie steak, new potatoes and fresh green peas, topped off with a mouth-watering dessert of strawberries and thick cream.

Melbourne's weather is noteworthy for its quick changes, alternating between hot and dry and cold and damp. The north wind, the *brick fielder* bringing down hot dry air from the interior plains, can push the mercury over the century mark. Then with startling suddenness, the cold southerly takes over. One day the thermometer reached 103 degrees F. at 3:00 p.m. Within twenty minutes the temperature dropped twenty-five degrees. This change took place without a *proper storm*. Only an abrupt swing in the wind and a few ridges of alto-cumulus clouds. Usually the cold front is heralded by a line of thunderstorms and then a day or two of rain or drizzle.

The Sabbath was the day to mount our bike and explore the country. Our first trip was to the Sir Colin Mackenzie Sanctuary at Healesville, where some of Australia's fauna, housed in spacious enclosures, appeared to be reasonably content. Many wild birds, attracted by their caged companions, were in view. While walking down woodland paths we encountered Fire-tailed Finches, Blue Wrens, King Parrots, White-napped Honeyeaters, Emus, kookaburras and kangaroos.

In Sherbrooke Forest, after an early morning's ride we found the incomparable lyrebird scratching for its breakfast in the leaf litter under

Rupert, the friendly Kookaburra.

a magnificent mountain ash, *Eucalyptus regnans*. [Individual trees of this species reach a height of over 300 feet. Trees felled in the early days of European settlement were reported to be over 400 feet tall!] Walking beneath the great trees we heard the familiar laugh of the kookaburra; but this time it was coming from the ground, which was unusual. Investigating, we found a lyrebird. While we watched, it mimicked the songs of several woodland birds before bursting into the unmistakable kook's laughter. In the forest we discovered several more lyretails while a dozen beautiful Crimson Rosellas flitted through the tree-tops. Unfortunately, lyrebirds display their tails only in the winter breeding season.

We took a day off work to allow us a two-day trip to Philip Island, home to Little Blue Penguins, mutton birds and koalas. The ride from Dandenong on the Bass highway was delightful. The flowering gum trees were in full bloom in colours ranging from white through pink to vivid scarlet. In the paddocks, flocks of Straw-Necked Ibis probed for grubs; while in the shrubbery Blue Wrens flashed and Bell Miners tinkled.

Just over the bridge at San Remo Ruth shouted, "Stop! I see a koala." I braked to a skid stop, propped the bike against a gum tree and we dismounted. As soon as the motor's noise stopped we realized we were in a swirl of birds and butterflies. We saw five species of butterfly and identified six kinds of birds.

Ruth said, "There's the koala," pointing to a ball of fur in the crotch of a thick gum tree. In a few minutes we discovered eighteen koalas, each in its own tree.

After a long session with the koalas we checked out a salt marsh on the other side of the island. It was an exciting bird bazaar with solid white masses of gulls and terns and a rim of hundreds of black cormorants covering the sand bars. In the scattered mangroves White Ibis sat in solemn groups while White-faced Herons stalked the shallows. A pair of Black-shouldered Kites occupied the top of a dead gum tree; a dozen Square-tailed Kites patrolled the shores. The water was shore-to-shore Black Swans in rafts of hundreds. To complete the scene a long line of a thousand curlews passed low overhead.

Although we were reluctant to leave the marsh, it was time to move on to the Penguin Parade. About eleven hundred Little Blue Penguins raise their young in burrows beneath the tussock grass on Philip Island. The birds emerge from the sea after dark and scramble up the beach with a crop load of fish for mates and young waiting in the nest holes. As the penguins have become a major attraction, a fence has been built on either side of the pathway to keep visitors from mingling with the birds. A string of electric lights illuminate the scene. Watchers line the barricades; penguins walk up the lighted path.

We had time for a cup of tea and a charred steak before the entertainment commenced.

It was dark now. The only sound: the swishing of the Bass Strait breakers on the sandy shore. Soon we were aware of ghostly bat-like forms sweeping around the lighted perimeter. These were mutton birds, Slender-billed Shearwaters, which nest here in burrows, like the penguins. Every year in late November they appear from the Southern Ocean, as punctual as Capistrano's swallows.

In the foam a cluster of little heads appeared, bobbed up and then vanished. Another group of heads and then six penguins stood upright, the light on their bellies making them look like white stakes. After a short hesitation they waddled closer only to be bowled over with the next incoming wave. More penguins materialized from the surf. Within minutes more than fifty were hurrying up the beach, most walking upright but a few *flat out*. When the vanguard reached the grass, sleek house-bound mates and fat downy chicks emerged and stood by the burrows to welcome the homecoming breadwinners. A cacophony of squawks, groans and moans from mutton birds and penguins were signs that everyone was happy with a seafood dinner. The rough, grassy slopes, apparently lifeless an hour ago now throbbed with activity.

We rode off to a sheltered dell in the high dunes and unrolled our sleeping bags for a night under the stars. After searching the area for burrows and finding none, we decided that we were beyond the colony. We wanted to leave the birds in peace. But we were only a dune away from the action. At ground level the cacophony seemed to intensify and the wings of low flying shearwaters brushed our faces. The joyful sounds (to hungry sea birds) slackened at midnight but it was bedlam again before dawn when the next shift was sent out. We are up early too, boiling the billy, while flocks of Silvereyes and Greenfinches chirped in the thorn bushes. Down on the rocks shags stretched their wings to catch the rays.

High in the blue, swirling groups of swifts greeted the sun. Underground, hundreds of penguins and mutton birds were sleeping.

We found a young orphan kookaburra on the ground two weeks before we left the farm. Although fully grown it was unable to fly. We were aware that young birds are best left alone as parents are often lurking nearby. For better or for worse, *keep well-meaning but usually lethal hands off*. A thorough, time-consuming search seemed to indicate we had a real orphan. And so we took it home intending to nourish it until it was able to fend for itself.

Rupert was given a perch in the corner over the woodbox. We fed him ground beef but he preferred his meat alive on the hoof. In order to satisfy his tastes and craving for vitamins and roughage we took him out on bush excursions after skinks, wolf spiders, dragonflies and other big game of the wild. A favourite meat shop was under the thick bark of pine stumps. Stationing Rupert on a strategic perch, we pried off a chunk of bark revealing a family of wolf spiders. Rupert was hopeless until one of the unlucky creatures twitched; then he was down in a flash snapping up, in his big Brazil-nut beak, anything moving. Our bird didn't swallow until the animal was properly dead and harmless. His method with spiders was a rapid pass back and forth through his mandibles, effectively reducing the booty to mincemeat. Lizards: he hammered the bejasus out of them until dead and tenderized. When the snack was prepared to Rupert's taste he threw back his head and with a series of choking ripples lunch disappeared. After a meal there was always a short beak wiping ritual.

Within a week Rupert could fly across the room. This presented new problems. We had to cover every square foot of our abode with newspapers every day, before we left to earn our bread, for Rupert never suffered from constipation. In fact, he excelled in high velocity defecation to the four winds and heaven and earth. Thank the lord for the daily newspaper!

At daybreak our bird began the routine of noisy preening and wing stretching; then flying practice. First, an awkward flapping from perch

And here is the 'Ah!' photo.

OK! I heard you the first time.

to the head of my bed and from there to the table. Sometimes I awakened to see a powerful beak glued to a large mound of feathers only an inch from my nose. On the table he stopped to shake his feathers and release a storm of dander and feather mites. Then he repeated the routine. Finally, he settled down to wait for breakfast after firing off a jet of whitewash. A kookaburra can't be housebroken.

Soon Rupert's nuisance value increased. He was now flying like a true aviator but still knocking over anything that wasn't nailed down. Worst of all he regarded the table as his personal territory. At mealtimes this was shattering. One day, while we had lunch, we stuck him outside on a perch by the window. We didn't see him leave. We made a cursory search outside. No Rupert.

At the end of the week we packed our gear and bade *goodbye* to the farm where we had spent forty back-stretching but happy days. At the top of the hill at the end of the road, we halted to look back on peaceful orchards, market gardens, groves of pine and eucalyptus and the distant blue Dandenong Ranges. We were seized by a bout of nostalgia. Suddenly a kookaburra darted down right at our feet and nabbed a four-inch lizard. It was Rupert – there was no mistaking those ragged tail feathers. He was living well in his native bush.

Five days later we walked away from the motorcycle shop on Queens Street, Melbourne, where our dusty old bike stood forlornly at the curb, like a faithful old horse on its last journey to the knackers yard. It was a sad sight. Tomorrow we would embark on a forty-day voyage to England on the *Castel Felice*. Sputnik had joined the stars in the night sky. It was the beginning of a new day for mankind.

DAVID STIRLING

Sandhurst, 1945　　　　　*New Zealand, 1956*

David Stirling was born in 1920 in Athabasca, Alberta. While growing up on a pioneer farm, he developed a keen interest in natural history: from butterflies and weather phenomena, to birds and botany. In World War II he served in the Canadian army in Canada and the UK, and graduated from the Royal Military College in Sandhurst, England, as a first lieutenant.

He married Ruth Carter in 1951. After working with the federal ministry of fisheries in Windsor and Winnipeg, they left on a two-and-a-half year journey around the world that included travelling by motorcycle, working at seasonal jobs and enjoying the natural world in New Zealand and Australia. On his return to Canada, he worked for the federal forestry ministry. He later moved to British Columbia Parks where he helped establish a nature interpretation and research program that was recognized as a model for other Canadian provinces.

At this time he became involved in the research and organization of overseas nature and wildlife tours. He led nature tours to Turkey, the Yukon, East Africa, the Galapagos Islands and other locations. After his retirement from BC Parks, David Stirling devoted more time to nature tours and travelled to Antarctica, the Russian Far East, the North West Passage and China.

David Stirling served on the boards of the American Birding Association, the Canadian Nature Federation and the Pacific Northwest Bird and Mammal Society. He helped in the founding of the Federation of British Columbia Naturalists. He was a member of International Council for Bird Protection, and is a member of The East Africa Wildlife Society and the Ornithological Society of the Middle East. He taught bird identification courses at Victoria's community college, and toured Canada and the United States with the National Audubon Society's wildlife films and Jim Bowers' wildlife presentations.

David Stirling received the Victoria Natural History Society's distinguished service award in 1989 and was given an honorary life membership in recognition of his long involvement with the society. He received Parks Canada's Interpretation Award of Merit in 1985. He was presented with the Queen's Jubilee Visit Medal in 2002 and also honoured in 2006 for his work with BC Parks. In 2008 he received the BC Field Ornithologists Award for ornithology.

Ruth Stirling died in 2002. Daughter Patricia, husband Cyril and their two children, Siobhan and Rory, live in Duncan, BC. David Stirling lives in Victoria, BC, Canada.

LaVergne, TN USA
29 October 2010

202818LV00001B/9/P